DEDICATION

To the young of present and future days, lest they forget the old.

My wife, Magda, and I during a visit to our daughters in the U.S.A. Autumn 1981.

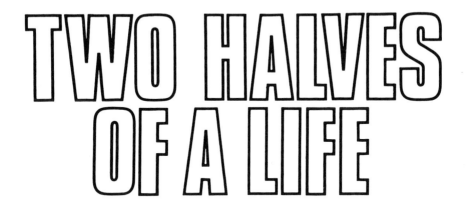

TWO HALVES OF A LIFE

By Dr K.F.M. Pole

MERESBOROUGH BOOKS
1982

Published by Meresborough Books,
7 Station Road, Rainham, Gillingham, Kent. ME8 7RS

ISBN 0905270 509

Printed and bound by Mackays of Chatham Ltd

CONTENTS

ACKNOWLEDGEMENTS

It is beyond me to mention all the people without whose help this book would never have been written; but for them I would have ended my life in a concentration-camp or fallen by the wayside later on. In neither case would I have had the opportunity or the material to write this.

I shall, therefore, confine myself to the last stages. The brunt of drafting the book with me and taking dictation fell still to Peggy Fox, my secretary for many years, but after her death Colleen Murphy, Beverley Weir and Judy Taffs most nobly rallied round to help with sorting, correcting, copying and dealing with correspondence. To all of them I owe many thanks.

Then there is Gerry Mancini who kindly mentioned my script to the publishers. To the publishers themselves I also owe many thanks; Hamish Mackay Miller could not have been more friendly, forthcoming and helpful.

Last but not least I want to thank my wife Magda whose only adverse reaction to my activities was to leave a copy of the "Daily Telegraph" conspicuously marked for me to read; the title of the relevant paragraph was "Doctors' work drives wives to drink". She never took to drink. Whether this was due to me keeping — if only just — on the right side of the borderline or to her own strength of character I must leave for others to judge.

Magda and I in Switzerland on our way to England.

Chapter 1
THE INVASION

It had been threatening for so long that most people no longer took the threat seriously. Even the violent assault that had been made by Germany ending with the assassination of Dollfuss, who was then Prime Minister (in Austria the equivalent title is "Chancellor") on July 12th, 1934 — though it had cost his life — left Austria intact. Thus there seemed at the time nothing particularly sinister in crowds thronging the streets in the centre of Vienna when my wife and I attended a lecture given by Bishop Gawlina, then Bishop of the Forces, who spoke at the "Kulturbund" on the problems of leadership in the State, the Forces and the Church. Looking back, I have the unforgettable memory of noise from the streets penetrating into the lecture hall, with members of the Vaterlaendische Front and Nazi sympathisers demonstrating and shouting abuse at each other. It was in strange contrast to the atmosphere inside the hall, where an elegant audience had assembled, many of the men wearing old Imperial uniforms.

But the next day it happened. I was at the time in general medical practice, my name was Karl Friedrich Pollaczek, and I was visiting patients when I was told in one house that it had just been announced on the radio that the Germans had invaded Austria and Chancellor Schuschnigg had decided against armed resistance in order to avoid spilling "the blood of brothers". At this stage I did not realise there was any danger to ordinary citizens like us, who were not involved in any political activities, but I did realise the danger to my godfather, Professor Dietrich von Hildebrand, who was high on the list of people wanted by the Gestapo. I telephoned him immediately, informing him what was happening, and he and his wife left at once by the frontier to the East, whilst the Germans marched in from the West. Even the Eastern frontier was already closed to Austrian citizens, but he — being a descendant of the distinguished Swiss family of sculptors — still held his Swiss citizenship and passport, besides his Austrian one. With this he could leave the country unhindered, though he and his wife in their haste could each take only one suitcase with them, and there was no time to contact their son who was ski-ing in the Austrian mountains.

Hildebrand had been Professor of Philosophy in Munich, and, when Hitler came to power, was offered by him the Chair of Philosophy, which he refused. He left for Austria where he was accepted as a Professor of Philosophy at the Vienna University. Very conscious that his strong Catholic beliefs were incompatible with everything the Nazis stood for, he took every opportunity to express his opposition to that regime. No wonder then that only a few hours after their arrival in Vienna the Gestapo looked for him in his home, unaware that he held double citizenship and consequently had been able to cross the frontier. They kept on looking for him, and when a few days later his son,

Franz, returned to Vienna, realised what had happened, and with his Swiss passport was leaving the country, the border guards checked him against a list of wanted people. They found his and his parents' names on it, and he was asked if they were relations of his. "I have no relations at all in Austria" was young Hildebrand's reply. This was perfectly true, as his relations had left, and his answer was very much in the spirit of his father who always held that under no circumstances must one tell a direct lie. I saw Hildebrand once more in Switzerland where in Fribourgh he took temporary shelter. He later emigrated to the U.S.A. obtaining a Professorship at the Graduate School of Fordham University. There he continued his work and had numerous books published. However, we never lost touch until his death in January 1977, when he was 87 years of age.

Knowing that Hildebrand was safe, my thoughts turned to the Rev. Johannes Oesterreicher, who ran a mission for the conversion of Jews in Vienna, and it was clear that he, as well as many of his pupils, were at risk; we spent that first evening together in his office burning files and papers which we realised must not fall into the hands of the Nazis.

Still I did not feel that there was any imminent threat to myself and my family, but the realisation that the old Austria no longer existed caused an indescribable sadness and strain. It was the only time in my life that I can remember having had three successive nights practically without sleep, and my wife and I decided to try and emigrate to escape the oppressive, almost stifling atmosphere in the country. Gradually we realised that there was also a threat to our personal freedom and safety as the news got around that people who did not give the Nazi salute were rounded up in the street, sometimes arrested, sometimes put to scrubbing the pavements or doing other, often senseless, jobs which were meant to be humiliating, while the onlookers sneered. Of course, any Jew or person considered to be Jewish (that is having one or more Jewish grandparents) — and that of course applied to us as converts to Catholicism — was forbidden to give the Nazi salute, not that we would have wanted to give it anyway. Even some of our friends who could — and according to Nazi mentality should — have given the Nazi salute, avoided it by walking out with a brief-case under one arm, and a parcel in the other hand. Thus they ensured that, having both hands occupied, they were unable to give the salute.

My sister-in-law was one of those rounded up in the street and put to scrubbing floors in some barracks, but she was fortunate in being afterwards released. My wife and I escaped being stopped in the street, she with a small child aged 3½ hardly ever going out, and I mainly moving by taxi which I could fortunately afford, particularly as I knew that I could not take any sizeable amount of money out of the country. I still managed to go on practising, and still had many patients coming to my consulting rooms. Many mothers came to me asking for advice as to what they should do about their children attending school; they were exhausted after having been taken near to the German/Austrian border at Salzburg, then back to Linz then on to Amstetten a little further inland, again back to St. Poelten and ultimately to Vienna. In each place they were made to cheer and jubilantly welcome the invaders. So much for the enthusiastic crowds which were shown on films welcoming the Fuehrer! And the flags, of course, his soldiers brought with them by the lorry-load.

An interesting patient was the former supplier of surgical instruments to our hospital. He rang me up, asking if I could see him late in the evening. "You did not know I was an active member of the National Socialist Party" he said, and explained that during the day he would have to be on duty in uniform in which he could not be seen visiting me, so he wanted to come after he could change into civilian clothes. Of course I consented. He was very friendly and offered help if ever I needed it saying that I had always been very decent to him and he appreciated it.

It soon became clear to me that I should not be able to continue much longer in general practice, and that my hospital appointments would come to an early end. I therefore asked for testimonials whilst the doctors under whom I had worked were still available, which I thought would not be for very long. I then started at once to arrange for emigration. The next weeks were, therefore, taken up with writing letters to England and the United States, to all people we knew who seemed likely to be able and willing to give us help in obtaining permits for immigration sending to them copies of my Curriculum Vitae and of various testimonials, particularly the last one which gave a fair summary of my various medical activities. It was signed by my senior Surgeon, and countersigned by the Superintendents of the two hospitals at which I held appointments. I certainly could not have asked for a better professional introduction. It said:- (in verbatim translation)

"Dr Karl Friedrich Pollaczek has been my Assistant at the Surgical Department of the First Public Sick Children's Institute since June 15th, 1934, and I approved his work in every respect so soon, and to such a degree, that when I took over also as Head of the Surgical Department at the Mariahilfer Clinic and Hospital, I wanted him to be there with me as well. Thus, Dr Pollaczek also came with me to that Hospital and was at first acting Assistant until, at the onset of 1936, he was officially appointed.

"Since then, Dr Pollaczek has been working in both places, and by his outstanding performance and his personal qualities has earned for himself in full measure the praise, confidence and affection of myself and the Superintendents of both hospitals.

"The activities of Dr Pollaczek, as my Assistant, were extremely varied. During those years he assisted me at many hundreds of major operations, and took his share in the after-treatment; he was frequently in sole charge of the Outpatients Department and, as well as dealing with the minor surgical cases which occurred there, he also performed major operations (appendicectomy, hernia/and cryptorchism operations) and acted as my substitute on his own whenever I was on leave, sick, or otherwise prevented from attending.

11

"In the Children's Institute I was able to initiate Dr Pollaczek into the specific aspects of children's surgery and thus, over the years, he became thoroughly familiar with this speciality. Moreover, for almost four years Dr Pollaczek was a well-nigh regular attender at the Outpatient Clinic of the Vienna Workmen's Insurance Company, and with the exceptionally large number — on average sixty patients a day — was able to observe and treat the damage and injuries caused under different work conditions. Here too, whenever I could not attend, Dr Pollaczek has been my deputy with full responsibility, which was very unusual, indicating the exceptional confidence not only of myself but also of the Board of the Insurance Company, because this task is normally reserved for Specialists and not entrusted to doctors in general practice; after all, because of their particular difficulties, such patients are frequently referred by general practitioners for expert opinion, advice and special treatment.

"Besides his work in the hospitals under my care, Dr Pollaczek was also in general practice, which he was enabled to do because, apart from the fixed Outpatient hours, he was not tied to any definite duty timetable. Through his activities in private general practice (which developed with gratifying speed, so that, although comparatively young, he is already one of the well-known doctors of Vienna) Dr Pollaczek has always maintained his contact with the other disciplines of medicine, which in turn benefited his surgical work in the hospitals when, during after-treatment, non-surgical complications occurred, and thus questions of diagnosis in border-line areas arose.

"From the very outset Dr Pollaczek brought to his work with me the best pre-conditions: a splendid comprehensive general medical education, which he acquired as House Surgeon and House Physician — and particularly also as acting Assistant in the Surgical Department — under eminent Professors of the Viennese school who headed the various departments of the State Hospital "Wieden". Moreover, his thorough grounding, working over the years in the theoretical disciplines of medicine, (Pathology, Bacteriology and related subjects) as well as his own research work fertilised his always lively interest in all clinical problems. Added to all this are the personal qualities of Dr Pollaczek: his absolute reliability, his energy, presence of mind, conscientiousness and exactitude in all his work, his dexterity, which made him an excellent and successful surgeon, his diagnostic gift which makes him appear born to be a doctor, his love and dedication to his vocation and to the sick, together with his friendliness, fellowship and trustworthiness. Thus Dr Pollaczek is equally loved and esteemed by his patients, colleagues, superiors and subordinates.

"As Dr Pollaczek was able — as no doubt is sufficiently obvious from this testimonial — to deepen his knowledge and experience over years in intensive and varied ways, thus continuously perfecting his training, he can be described as a doctor with quite outstanding qualifications.

"I give him for his future life which, because of his plans may soon separate him from me, all my good wishes. I am convinced that his way will lead him to future successes, but all the same I shall deeply regret losing him as a close work companion because he is an exemplary assistant, colleague and deputy and, moreover, has become a dear personal friend to me."

In America, Miss Lina Newton of Philadelphia, an old friend of my parents-in-law, was eager and probably sufficiently influential to provide help. However, from the very beginning, England was our first choice. Austrians always felt a particular affinity with the Anglo-Saxons. There is some truth in what Count Czernin wrote in his book "This Salzburg" about Austrians. "We are fearful snobs about everything Anglo-Saxon; as a matter of fact some say we go too far. If you talk English we will pull ourselves to bits for you. God knows why. If, after a week's acquaintance, you ask us whether we were born or brought up in England, as our English is so perfect, we will willingly die for you."

There seemed to be a good chance for admission to England. My father-in-law, Egon Wellesz, a Professor of the History of Music at Vienna University and a well known composer, had been made an honorary Doctor of Music at Oxford University in 1932. He happened to be in Holland — where a concert of his was being performed — when the Germans occupied Austria. Warned by us he was wise enough not to return, but went on to Oxford where he was invited by friends and accepted with open arms in University circles. He was given a Readership in Byzantine music — the field in which he had established his fame — and made a fellow of Lincoln College. In Austria Egon was evidently on the list of suspects though I do not know for certain why; perhaps because he was known to be a monarchist. Anyway, one day when we visited my wife's mother two men from the Gestapo arrived, searched the house and asked about his whereabouts, but left again — seemingly for the present satisfied — with the information that he was abroad because of some concert performances.

Egon's honorary Doctorate, and the friends he had made in England, would, we felt certain, reassure the authorities about our personal integrity. We also had many influential sponsors. In particular there was Harry Colles who, on the same day as Egon, had been made an honorary Doctor of Oxford; he and his wife Hester later became our main protectors. Another was the Hon. Mrs Lyell, whose son, Lord Charles Anthony Lyell, (later killed in action and awarded the V.C.), came to see us in Vienna and took out some of our Austrian jewellery, which we might have had difficulty in getting past the frontier check. One was at that time still allowed to take jewellery in accordance with one's "social status", but the interpretation of this was very much at the discretion of the German Customs Officials.

The usual practice when a refugee was admitted to Britain, was that his whole family should be given refuge, and we had at that time already one small daughter. My medical qualifications too, and my past medical history, made me a likely candidate for one of the fifty admissions offered to Austrian doctors, of whom I was told 950 had applied. Of course we were admitted only for the purpose of studies, and had to re-qualify before being admitted to the Medical Register. The actual selection of the refugees was to take some time, but meanwhile we obtained visitors' visas, and based on this were certain to get transit visas through France and Switzerland. As we had relatives there who guaranteed that we would not be a burden to the country, our Swiss visas were to be for transit with permission to stay for up to three months.

At last, everything appeared ready for our application to emigrate, and it was then that the full misery of the would-be emigrants dawned on me for the first time. There was a long queue of applicants and there was evidently no hope to even be admitted to the office the same day. As a matter of fact I was told that applicants usually queued round the nearest street corner from 5 o'clock in the morning, and as soon as queueing at the door of the Passport Office was permitted, started running towards it. Those who were fairly near the front of the queue when the Office closed were sometimes given a paper which entitled them to priority admission the next day, but there was no guarantee of that.

My information came from a policeman who was on duty regulating the queue when I got to the Passport Office. In the mood of those days one was willing to try anything, however little chance of success it seemed to offer, so I went up to the Officer and told him of my predicament, that I was a doctor, still in practice, and thus could not spend days on end queueing. What was I to do? I was fortunate in coming up against the right man. Feeling unobserved he looked sympathetically at me and said "Don't come tomorrow, I shall not be on duty, but I shall be here the day after. Come at 10 o'clock and I shall let you in by a side door". He was as good as his word, and a few minutes after my arrival I found myself in the corridors of the Passport Office. Even then it was still a fairly long wait but I felt very fortunate hearing other people talk about their having queued for days on end, and some for up to a week. At last I was in the office itself and handed in my passport, together with a document certifying that there were no charges against me and that I had fulfilled all my tax obligations. It seemed a big step forward.

A few days later I received notification that our passports were ready for collection.

This time there was only a moderate queue, but when I arrived at the desk I was told that our passports could not be found, would I come back another day. The bottom seemed to have fallen out of my world, but what could we do? Very downhearted, my wife and I started to descend the nearest staircase, one of the many in the huge Police headquarters of which the Passport Office occupied a part. We had not gone down many steps when we met a lady coming up. She was a welfare worker who knew us superficially through her elder sister, a great friend of my wife's mother. "What are you doing here?" she asked, and we explained that we intended to emigrate, that we had come to collect our passports but they had been lost. "Come back with me" she said, "I shall see if I cannot get them to make another search", and a few minutes later we had our passports with the necessary exit permits in our hands.

It was only later that I was told that this losing the passport was a favourite game of the Officers, who expected a little recompense in money for having another look. At that time I was too innocent to realise it, and anyway would not have dared to offer anything which would really have constituted a bribe, for fear of landing us in more serious trouble. Anyway, it seemed almost miraculous that this lady should come up the same staircase of the many there were in our very minute of need. I have been a strong believer in guardian angels ever since, and many of the later events confirmed my belief.

On we went to the British Embassy to collect our visitors' visas. They were just about to close the door when we arrived, but I had been given a visiting card by the Hon. Mrs Lyell with an introduction written on it which I showed to the porter, and he let us pass. To get the visas took only a few minutes, as they were in readiness for us, and somewhat exhausted, but happy and hopeful, we went home.

We had air tickets for two days hence, and it seemed a foregone conclusion that the transit visas through France and Switzerland would be obtained without difficulty. Freedom seemed near and that night we had a peaceful sleep, when at about 6.30 a.m. there was a knock on our bedroom door and our maid said there was a gentleman who wanted to see me. This unexpected knock at the door was something one had feared for many weeks, but at this stage we thought we had escaped it. We had not. A young man in civilian clothes stood in front of the bedroom door, identified himself as an officer of the Gestapo, and said that he had orders to arrest me. When I asked why he replied that he did not know, those were his orders. However, personally he seemed a rather nice young man, an Austrian who evidently did not like his job. From the first moment he tried to be helpful, and was willing to wait not only while I dressed, but also while I telephoned several people telling them what had happened. Towards him I took the attitude that there must be a mistake, as I had the day before received permission to emigrate, and he seemed willing to play along with that.

Though cases were known in which Gestapo officers tore up passports, I felt I had no choice but to hand him my passport as proof, and I also trusted my impression of him as a benevolent and honest man. I was right. On the way to the local police station, which served as a branch office of the Gestapo, he told me the best he could do for me was to have a preliminary formal interview; then we would have to wait for the Superintendent's further decisions.

I was known at the local police station because I had lived in that district of Vienna for a long time, and also had been a doctor at the local hospital. I was taken into a large room containing several desks, each with a plain clothes officer sitting behind and an arrested man standing in front. My officer took me to the one which was vacant and I was offered a chair, which I do not think had ever happened to a prisoner there before or since. Suddenly, the officer sat bolt upright and said in a sharp voice, which I am sure could be heard all over the room, "You will tell me now the truth, the whole truth and nothing but the truth, and if you do not do so you will be made to feel the severity of the Gestapo". Settling back in his chair he added under his breath "This is a formality doctor". This made me feel very much better.

15

I cannot now remember what I was asked nor what I answered. It was certainly the truth, but I don't think the full truth! After the interview, the officer said "I now have to take you to the cell until the Superintendent arrives". The next stop was at the jailer's, where I had to empty my pockets, and there was undoubtedly a look of surprise in his eyes when I put my rosary on his table. I also had to deposit my tie, belt and suspenders, obviously to prevent me from hanging myself in the cell. There would not have been any fear of that, not only because it is not my line, but also because the small cell was filled with prisoners who had been rounded up during the night; there was standing room only.

Naturally there was an air of despondency, but after the previous day's experience I still had hope that all would come right. About half an hour elapsed, mainly in silence, everyone occupied with his own thoughts, then the cell door opened and my name was called. It was the officer who had arrested me and he took me to the Superintendent who had just arrived. He looked at my passport, which confirmed my story that I had the previous day received permission to emigrate. "It must all be a mistake" I maintained, "the orders to arrest me must have been given before I received the permit". "When do you leave the country?" the Superintendent asked, and I replied truthfully "I have air tickets for the day after tomorrow. I still have to get transit visas for France and Switzerland". "Go and arrange your affairs" was the reply, and handing back the passport to me he added "Meanwhile I shall ask in the Central Department of the Gestapo what to do about you". I thanked him, and was taken back to the jailer, where I collected my belongings and, once more at liberty, I hurried home.

Here I found that my wife had a visitor. Father Robert John, an old friend of ours from the Hildebrand circle had, evidently, some forebodings that all was not well, and came to see how we were getting on. I told my wife and him quickly what had happened, shaved — the one thing I had not had time to do before being taken to the police station — and left for the French Embassy to collect our transit visas. I had been given the name of an official there whom I should see, so I took little notice of the long queue outside one of the doors, but went to another entrance and told the porter that I had an appointment to see the said official, whose name I can no longer recall. The porter pointed to the queue and said "All these people have an appointment to see him, you had better go to the end of the queue".

With the length of the queue it was quite clear to me that I would not even get inside the Embassy that same day, and once more all seemed lost. Still there was nothing else I could do, so I waited in the queue, racking my brains for a way out. After all, every delay was likely to mean being re-arrested by the Gestapo and I realised that, though I myself had never been involved in politics, the fact that all my friends — and above all my godfather — were very active anti-Nazis would come to light.

I was still standing, trying to puzzle out possibilities, when the door opened, the porter called my name and when I came up to him said "There is someone to see you". As I entered the hall Father John, whom I had left at home with my wife, was standing there. "I went by the Embassy" he said "to see if you were all right and when I saw you near the end of the queue I realised what was happening. I thereupon rang the Embassy Chaplain, who is a friend of mine, told him about you and asked if I could use his name to get you seen; after all it could easily be a matter of life and death". The porter had become very helpful. Though I was told it was impossible to get the visas earlier than in three days, as they had to be confirmed from Paris, he put his Lodge with the telephone at my disposal and I rang everybody I could think of with French connections who might be willing to help. To cut a long story short, after two hours I walked out of the Embassy with the visas in our passports.

By taxi to the Swiss Embassy, where things went as I had expected, and after ten minutes our passports were completed with all necessary endorsements. A taxi again, this time to the travel agency, and our air tickets for the day after the morrow were changed for train tickets the same evening.

Home again, for hasty packing, suitcases and one trunk. I rang our removers, a small private firm who had worked for our family for many years and three generations, arranged with them that they would pack up our other things and send what they could after us. I understood that all freight could be paid in Austrian money up to the London Docks, and I left authority with them to receive payment out of the money I had to leave behind. I could easily be "generous" as I knew that all money left in Austria was lost anyway, and I was only allowed to take with me, for my wife, our small daughter aged 3½ and myself, the equivalent of £3.10s. I also gave our maid some extra money on condition that she packed and removed her things the same morning. I next spoke to the porter of the house in which we had our flat: "You know what happened this morning?" I asked him. He and his family had been patients of mine and he nodded knowingly and sympathetically. "In case anybody asks for me I won't be home before 10 o'clock in the evening" I instructed him. Once again I had told the truth if not the full truth. I was not home before 10 o'clock but I was not at home afterwards either. We left our house by taxi and went to my wife's mother, on the way leaving our trunk at the Station. It was June 20th, 1938, my wife's birthday, and at 9 o'clock in the evening we left Vienna by train.

Naturally we were still tense, but at the frontier everything went smoothly. Though my wife was bodily searched by a woman Customs Officer and the luggage inspected, there was no objection to our passing through. The feeling of relief when we had entered Switzerland was indescribable. However uncertain the future, we felt we were free at last, and could do something ourselves to shape it. I never imagined then how marvellous the new life would eventually be. I was only aware that it was an entirely new life which lay before us. The old life had ended in what seemed to be a disaster for us, and indeed was a disaster for many people, but for ourselves we had much good to remember and be thankful for from earlier days.

My mother's parents.

My father's father.

My father's mother.

Chapter 2
THE FAMILY HISTORY TO MY FATHER'S DEATH

I was born with the proverbial "silver spoon" in my mouth, my family being one of relative wealth and which, for a Jewish family, played an unusually important role in contemporary society. But my parents were not happy.

From some of my mother's autobiographical notes I found among papers which happened to come to me in England, I know more about her family than my father's.

My great-grandfather, in the female line, was a cloth merchant who had inherited the business from his father. His firm provided cloth for the Austrian Army in the Napoleonic wars, and he had an official letter of thanks for the "excellent service" they provided, which was dated 1810. He lived on the out-skirts of Prague, then the second city of the Austro-Hungarian Empire, and seems to have always done well for himself and his family, but became really wealthy when he won the big prize in one of the official lotteries. With the money he was able to fulfil the dream of every provincial, which was to move to the capital, Vienna, and have his children educated there, which was done very well, and successfully. When later he lost his money in share dealings, his children, in return, looked after him lovingly and respectfully.

This great-grandfather, Hermann Taussig, had four children. One of the daughters married a prosperous, but by no means eminent, man; the other daughter achieved only one distinction in that she became my grandmother! The two sons, however, made rather interesting careers. The younger, Emil, was apparently gay and charming, and loved by his nieces, but was something of a gambler. He fell in love with a Christian girl but the family refused to agree to the marriage. Sometime later, when he contracted gaming debts, the family settled them but made him move to Munich where, at that time, electricity came into use. Starting as an electrical fitter, he eventually became director of the Munich Electricity Company, and consequently was again acknowledged by the family. He died at the age of 57.

The elder son, Theodor, however, became the pride, centre and head of the whole family. When still quite young he became a director of the Imperial Bank and later its Governor; among other high positions he was also President of the State Railway Company, and, remarkable for an unbaptised Jew, received high decorations, and with them a Knighthood, which in Austria was hereditary. My mother evidently did not like this uncle, because she considered him pompous. He expected the children in the family to kiss his hand, and when one day my mother realised that his children did not kiss her father's hand, she declined, and shook his hand instead. Ever since that incident there seemed to have been a certain amount of hostility between them. My mother also resented the fact that

19

any marriage in the family had to be approved by him, and that his approval was guided less by the prospective spouse's character than by social and financial considerations. However, he himself married for love, a girl without means.

My mother's paternal grandfather was a mercer, dealing mainly with brocades, His family too seems to have been well-to-do, and my grandfather was a promising young man who wanted to be an architect, and is supposed to have been talented in that direction. His parents, however, wanted him to go into banking. At the age of 28, when he married, he was already director of a bank, but soon afterwards it went into liquidation. He then went into private banking, and remained fairly well-off, but the loss of his position, which made him the relatively unsuccessful poor relation in the very rich and pompous circle of the family Taussig, seems to have made him lose his self-confidence, for he was later inclined to self-pity, and was always "nannied" by his wife. He had two sisters, one of whom was married to a doctor to whom my mother, in her autobiography, referred as the best man she ever met in her life. He had a few rich patients, but in the main his enormous practice was among the poor on the outskirts of Vienna. His patients adored him, and my mother tells of his funeral at which one of the main streets of his district was crowded with mourners, many of whom were in tears. I have no doubt that my mother's admiration for her uncle, which she often expressed, played a great part in my thinking, from an early age, of the medical profession as something very special and desirable.

My mother was the eldest child, after a still-born baby; then another girl, Anna, was born, and a brother who died at the age of 4 from scarlet fever. Afterwards there were two more boys, Otto and Fredi. The grandparents lived all their married life in the same flat which, when the children were born, was enlarged by taking in the neighbouring flat.

My mother was said to have been a dreamer as a child, and in many respects remained so all her life. She was very attached to her grandfather Taussig who, for a time, lived with them, and out of love for him, who seems to have been the last practising Jew in the family, she herself went through a brief "Jewish period". Her mother is said to have had a hidden poetic and soft streak, but the trait she showed mainly, and which I best remember, was one of efficiency and coolness, probably explained by the fact that her mother died when she was 14 years old, and her father expected her to take over the responsibilities of the household.

In my grandparents' house Christmas presents were exchanged, but there was no formal celebration with a tree, because of grandmother's father who thought it was ridiculous for Jews to have a Christmas tree. But there was always a tree at the younger Taussig's, who, however, also celebrated the Jewish feast of Purim with an annual fancy-dress tea.

The whole extended family did things very much together. Summer holidays were taken in groups, very often in or near Ischl, which was fashionable because the Emperor had his summer villa there. There was a very distinctive artistic streak in the family. My mother was herself, apparently, very gifted in singing, acting and painting, but to her regret always remained an amateur. Her sister too

20

wrote some novels and poetry, and did some acting within the family. Her brother, Otto, who later became a respected lawyer, loved music, particularly chamber music, and having been taught by the Leader of the Vienna Philharmonic Orchestra became a very proficient violinist. The younger brother was a talented painter, but he never achieved great professional success. Acting played a considerable part in the family entertainments. Sometimes the children acted charades, sometimes they improvised scenes or acted plays written by members of the family, and birthdays especially were celebrated with plays sometimes written for the occasion.

A highlight which shows the extravagance of those days – almost unbelievable today – was a ball at Taussig's under the title "Puppenfee". This word means "dolls fairy", and was the name of a ballet being newly performed at that time in the Imperial Opera House. For the decoration of the ballroom the actual ballet scenery was hired from there. My mother played the part of the Japanese doll performing a fan dance, and for this she was given an embroidered silk kimono, which is still among my wife's possessions today.

When great-grandfather fell ill, he was nursed at home by a valet and two professional nurses, and it was not unusual for the family doctor to stay the whole night. Eventually he died, and at his funeral full Jewish ceremonies were celebrated in the family for the last time.

In their younger years the girls had governesses. My mother was on bad terms with all the governesses, and was much relieved when she reached an age where she required only teachers for a sort of finishing course at home, while the only governess in the house then was a French-Swiss, Mademoiselle Lily, whose task was really to look after the youngest brother and, at the same time, to keep a controlling eye on the girls. My mother got on very well with her; she became her confidante, and often actually helped her when she wanted to send letters or to meet young men behind her parents' backs.

In those days my mother fell in love with a young medical student, an episode to which she always referred as that of her great love, but which ended when her parents found out and she was locked up in her room until young Boris disappeared from the scene. Though of good family, as a student and without means he was not considered a suitable life partner.

At the many house parties my mother had opportunities to get to know famous actresses which greatly stimulated her interest in the theatre, in art, acting and writing. It was on New Year's Day, 1896, that she met Arthur Schnitzler at a party for the first time, having known him previously by sight only. He and Hugo von Hofmannsthal were great friends, and later came frequently to the grandparents' house. My mother was fascinated by them both, but whilst she and Hofmannsthal apparently actually flirted and kissed, she was more impressed by Schnitzler whom she found "a very trustworthy, interesting, elderly man" with whom she had long literary discussions. Her parents, however, were rather suspicious of Arthur Schnitzler, because of the plays "Anatole" and "The Liebelei" he had written which were considered rather frivolous. Hofmannsthal

21

Arthur Schnitzler in 1897, when he came to my grandparents' house.

and Schnitzler became the leading authors of their time, whose fame spread far beyond their native country. Hofmannsthal had the more lyrical leanings, writing poems, plays and librettos, whilst Schnitzler wrote plays and novels mainly on socio-psychological themes. He had qualified as a doctor before becoming a full-time author.

It is difficult to sort out exact dates, as my mother always tried to make herself younger, and referred to herself as being 17 years old when, now that I know her birthdate, she must actually have been about 21. However, I suppose she was 18 or perhaps 19 when she "came out", and between January and the end of March attended eighteen house balls and many other parties. Girls of her society went only very rarely to public balls, and during the time before her marriage she actually only attended two such very exclusive occasions. The big occasion in my grandparents' house was a party at which the young people performed a play set in a snowscape for which the necessary machinery was, once again, hired from the Imperial Opera House. As one can see, the standard of life was very high, but it strained my grandparents' resources to the full, and they were, therefore, increasingly anxious to have my mother "cared for" by marriage.

22

About this time my mother wrote a sketch called "Mimi", in which she casti-
gated the custom of arranged marriages. With the help of Hofmannsthal, who
actually wrote a prologue to the play, it was secretly arranged to have this play
published and it was accepted, with the proviso that it should first appear in a
periodical. However, an informer told the grandparents that the pseudonym in
the magazine covered their eldest daughter; a domestic storm broke, the further
publication of the play was stopped, and my mother was once again locked up
in her room.

After these experiences my mother herself became desirous of marriage, but
anyone who presented himself had to get the consent of Theodor Taussig, and
several were rejected.

Meanwhile, another summer came which the family spent in Alsace. During
their stay, heavy floods occurred, in the clearing up of which the military assisted.
Thus, for a short while, officers appeared on the scene. Although they soon
disappeared again, it seems that my mother's liking for young officers – who
later played a part in the life of the young widow – dates back to that time.

It was about this time that Otto Pollaczek appeared on the horizon; a young
man who had asked to be introduced to the family, and who was considered a
likely suitor. However, he had just gone to Ostend and Paris, and was not expected
back in Vienna until the autumn. Meanwhile my mother was sent on a visit to
Berlin. One of the Taussig daughters had married Wassermann, a young scientist
who achieved fame as the discoverer of the Wassermann reaction, and they lived
there. My mother had a great time with them, and in a rather flippant letter she
enquired of her parents whether Mr P. had, meanwhile, appeared "or anybody
else – it does not really matter".

At the end of her stay my mother was collected by Uncle Theodor who also
had been in Berlin on some business. It seems to have been the only time she was
alone with him for several hours, and certainly it was the only time she travelled
in his special coach which, for him as President of the Railway Company, was
hooked on to any train in which he wished to travel. In this coach he usually
took to holiday resorts his whole family, which eventually consisted of three
sons and nine daughters, plus governesses and numerous staff. On this occasion,
however, there were only Theodor Taussig, his valet, his secretary and my mother
travelling.

After her return to Vienna, an outing to the Prater was arranged where a
mutual friend was to introduce Otto P. The Prater, on the outskirts of Vienna,
once hunting grounds and pleasure park of the Emperor, was opened to the
public as a recreation area in the second half of the 18th century. I am not
certain, but should think it would include now, various sports establishments; in
the days of my youth it consisted only of two distinct parts. The elegant park
area had, running through the whole length of its centre, a chestnut tree-lined
main avenue, where flower parades were held and where, in fine weather, the
ladies in their carriages "took the air" making sure that their rivals would see
their new dresses and hats. They often interrupted their drives in the Krieau for

a "fork breakfast" (the mid-morning break) which consisted of something like cold Prague ham, boiled eggs and, usually, ice-cold milk. Alongside the main avenue were three fashionable restaurant-coffee houses where the rich often dined. Each of these places had its band, the most famed of which, at one time, was that of Johann Strauss. To both sides of the central avenue paths ran between beautiful wide spaces of bush and meadow where wild flowers grew; there the children of the middle classes were often taken for walks. When the carriage could be spared by our parents, my brother and I, with our governess, were frequently taken to the Prater, and leaving the carriage, went for a walk through the meadows, meeting the carriage again lower down the main avenue. I well remember in the season the coachman, whilst waiting for us, carved little mushrooms out of chestnuts, which he gave us and we proudly took home.

Quite separate from this was "the people's Prater", a large and elaborate amusement park with merry-go-rounds, slides, Punch and Judy shows, a scenic railway, haunted houses, and trains winding their way slowly through artificial dimly-lit caves. It was surmounted by the famous giant Ferris wheel, which was — and I believe still is — one of the landmarks of the Vienna skyline. This part of the Prater was a paradise for children, but even more so for soldiers and servant girls who, on Sunday afternoons and warm evenings, thronged the place, and for students who took their "sweet girls" there for an evening out, ending with a meal in one of the several taverns, dance halls or cafés.

It was October 7th, 1897, when my grandmother, with her two daughters and an Italian governess, went to the Krieau, and the introduction duly took place. After the refreshments my grandmother returned home in her carriage, while the girls, the young man and the governess went for a bicycle ride, the girls' bicycles evidently being kept permanently in a garage in the Prater. My mother was obviously not very much taken with her future husband, and complained in her diary that on this first meeting he had said that, if he got married, he would expect blind obedience from his wife. However, she had to admire his carriage, which was more luxuriously equipped than any other she knew of at that time. When asked at home how she found him, she replied "Terrible", and when asked the reason, she said "Because of his view of the world", to which her parents answered "Not everybody can have the views of Arthur Schnitzler".

Another "domestic catastrophe" occurred in the family at this time, concerning mother's sister, Anna, who had fallen in love with Felix Salten who, being poor and unknown at that time, was flatly rejected by her parents. Later he became the famous author of "Bambi". The separation of the two was enforced by the usual routine of locking up and tears, but they never forgot their love for one another, and when, later on, each got married, my aunt called her first son Felix, and he called his daughter Anna.

Consequently my mother decided to leave home at all costs, and started to flirt with her future husband which, as she said, brought out the best in him. However, he did not declare himself as quickly as she had expected, partly because he first wanted to liquidate some still-remaining romantic entanglements,

Father about 1897.

and partly because of difficulties with his father who was afraid that, entering the circle of the Taussigs would make his son — who was already inclined to extravagance — more extravagant than ever. However, on February 17th, 1898, the old man himself, on behalf of his son, came to my mother's parents to ask for her hand.

My father's father, Wilhelm, was then the head of the firm, with his younger brother as partner. They were the largest rawhide dealers in the old Austrian/ Hungarian monarchy. The firm had been founded by his father Isaak Zacharias, who, at the age of about 40, seems to have moved from his birthplace in Kolin to Prague, then the capital of Bohemia and the second city of the empire. From there the family moved to Vienna when my father was 2 years old. Not having any diaries of my father's to consult, I know much less of his family than of my mother's, and have to rely on verbal information and some documents. From these I know that grandfather Wilhelm was married to Charlotte of the family Loew-Beer. They had been given a citizen's coat-of-arms, published in the 11th book, page 55 of the European Collection of Coat-of-Arms from the year 1690. This was a rare distinction for Jews; how it came about I do not know, but

25

Mother in 1902.

evidently the Loew-Beers were a respected family. On a visit to Prague, I saw
their family tomb in the old Jewish cemetery. I also know from my mother's
notes, that both the firm and my grandfather Wilhelm were held in high regard;
my grandfather — in spite of his considerable wealth — led a very modest life, a
tendency obviously not shared by his son, Otto.

During the winter of their engagement, my father happened to be the Chairman of the Committee arranging the annual Ball of the Viennese Merchants, and
consequently my mother found herself on the platform with all the VIP's. There
she was introduced to the Grand Duke Ludwig Victor, younger brother of the
Emperor, who commented "This is the sweetest little bride I ever saw" — a
remark which my mother said in her memoirs was quoted next day in the daily
papers. He sent the engaged couple a golden set of mocca pot, milk jug and sugar
basin, as a wedding gift, which I still remember seeing in a glass show-case with
his letter of congratulations in a drawer underneath, but which has since been
lost, as have so many other family possessions.

My mother was at first disappointed that they were to live in the second
district of Vienna, which was not considered to be "a good address". However, it
was my father's own house, and was the usual type of Viennese town house, with
two flats to each storey. The owner usually had his flat on the first floor, and
when the family grew, united the two neighbouring flats into one large one. This
is what happened in my parents' case, and when my mother had the staircase
embellished with a red stair carpet, wrought iron chandelier and green plants, she
no longer minded the district. Moreover, the house and the firm's office house
backing on to it, where my father's father lived, and where also the stores were
situated, was conveniently placed near the railway station, which was used for
most of the trade, and also close to the Prater.

26

The marriage was originally planned for April, but had to be postponed because great-grandfather Loew-Beer died; it eventually took place on May 10th, 1898.

Before the birth of her first child, my elder brother, my mother wrote a letter to her husband in case she should die in childbirth. In this letter she said she would destroy it if she survived; she never did, but copied it into her autobiography. In this letter she asked that the child should be taught to believe in God and prayer, but not religious ceremonies.

My father was overjoyed to have a son and for a time it seemed that he and mother got on well, earlier friction having been smoothed over. However, this did not last long; disagreements reoccurred, and on the second anniversary of their marriage my mother wrote a letter purporting to be in the name of her son, congratulating father, and at the same time giving vent to her own various disappointments and complaints as it were through the baby's mouth. I am afraid mother never got away from play-acting even in her daily life, and her literary inclinations always came to the surface, often with unfortunate results. Thus she wrote one sketch entitled "Happy Marriage — a Tragedy in Innumerable Parts" which evidently depicted one of the many scenes and discussions which took place. In it she mentions herself as saying, among other things, "You are not worthy to touch the child", enumerating all his faults and complaints, while my father stretched out on the couch and, during her sermon, went to sleep. It is also evident from her diaries that she disliked all his friends, and complained that he did not discuss everything with her. However, he made it clear in one letter to her that he did not feel he had her support, and that she was not a woman with whom he could discuss business worries. It was at this time that his mother, to whom he was very attached, and who had been ailing for some time, died of cancer; my mother was very irate when she came across a letter father wrote to a former girl friend saying that she was the only one to whom he could talk about his sorrow at the loss of his mother, and with whom he could discuss other worries.

Evidently mother distrusted father from the very beginning, and in the summer of 1902, suspected him of saying, out of jealousy, detrimental things about the character of her sister Anna's prospective husband: they later turned out to be quite correct. He was a civil servant from a good and wealthy family, but in later years when an investigation about alleged interference with boys threatened, he committed suicide.

I was born on December 22nd, 1902. I was a very big and placid baby, and always able to occupy myself without troubling anyone, in marked contrast to my brother, who wanted a lot of attention. On my birthday, my father gave mother a ring with a large emerald "as a reward", a remark she took badly, complaining in her memoirs that this sounded like payment to a bought woman.

My father's financial situation appears to have been very good indeed; my mother mentions a budget of about 100,000 Kronen a year. We then had an eight-roomed flat with a butler-valet, lady's maid, chamber-maid, cook, kitchen-maid and a governess, and when she travelled that summer with us boys to the seaside, mother took her maid, a wet-nurse, and a governess with her. And, of course, there was the carriage. Like all those who had no stables my father did not actually own the carriage, but it was on permanent hire. It was at his disposal whenever required, always the same carriage — which could be used open or closed — the same pair of handsome horses, and the same coachman. It was up to the customer to provide any special equipment, and my father's was said to be particularly luxurious.

At the beginning of November 1903, my mother came across a letter addressed to my father signed "Once your Hasi" (Pet Rabbit), and, though the very signature showed that this was but a shadow of the past, and my father tried to explain this, she said she would leave him at the beginning of the New Year. In spite of all father's pleading and protestations of love, and the threat that he would commit suicide if she left him, she locked her bedroom door against him.

However, the marriage carried on, if uneasily, and when in the spring of 1905, fire destroyed our drawing room, and with it a precious and highly insured tapestry, my mother was for a time happily occupied with arrangements for refurnishing it, largely with the insurance money. She found this task very stimulating, but refers to herself as being in those days "two persons in one".

My mother writes in her memoirs that she did not like the drawing room or the sitting room as they were originally, but she then furnished both rooms with antique furniture, and this is how I remember them, not having any recollection of their original state. The drawing room had a white marble fireplace and Empire furniture upholstered with red and gold embroidered brocade, the walls being covered with the same material. In place of the tapestry that was destroyed, some hundred or more miniatures, which my father had collected over the years, hung on a dark velvet background. The sitting room was furnished with Marie Therese furniture of which two tables and some chairs came to me in England, where I eventually had to sell them. There was a large oil painting of the young Empress, Elizabeth, wife of the almost legendary Francis Joseph — (Kaiser Franz Joseph). It is now hanging in our dining room in England.

The marriage dragged on, partly because neither father nor mother was willing to part from the children. My mother writes that in those days she spent much time in the nursery with us, but strangely I have no recollection of this; in my memory we appear to have been looked after mostly by governesses and later in part by teachers.

In those days mother seems to have taken increasingly to social life, meeting many people known in the art world, and young officers from noble families. Father did not seem to mind, as he is quoted as saying "Every titled man who is introduced to my wife courts her", and as having given her a copy of the Gotha, the German language equivalent of Debrett. There is no doubt that my mother was anxious to observe all the proprieties, but the marriage apparently never again became a real marriage, and now my mother had real reason to blame father for infidelity. One affair with a married woman caused widespread gossip, and eventually a provisional agreement for separation and maintenance was

My mother in 1906.

made. However, my father protested that he loved only her, and in the end mother consented once more to a reconciliation, and together they went on a "second honeymoon", a journey to Italy on which they visited the crater of Vesuvius as the last visitors before that year's great outbreak of the volcano. But as to the marriage, the holiday was not a success.

Mother had made friends with a couple who had a big estate in the country where they gave hunting parties. During her stay there she left us in the care of an Austrian kindergarten nurse who, in autumn 1906, had replaced our former English governess, Miss Peters, as it was thought time that we became fluent again in our native language which we had almost forgotten. Father was to supervise us, and though my mother doubted it he must have done so, because I remember playing in his room. I was altogether very attached to him, though he was frequently away on business journeys and now my recollection is mainly like snapshots, seeing him and me in particular situations. That autumn and winter 1906/7 saw further changes in our flat. The entrance space was transformed into a real entrance hall with baroque furniture, and in the dining room, which had English style mahogany furniture, the wallpaper was replaced by covering the walls with white stucco. Both parents were much involved in social life and gave a party in our flat for 65 people with a dinner supplied by Sacher, the top restaurant in the City; during that evening my mother and her sister danced a ballet, coached by a ballet master from the Imperial Opera.

My father in 1908.

In contrast to this period in which father seems to have been particularly prosperous, it was as soon afterwards as August 1907, that for the first time he wrote to my mother about business difficulties and said that for economy's sake the carriage would have to be given up. However, three days later he counter-manded this order because he thought diminishing his staff would make the bank suspicious.

My mother again found love letters to father which indicated that there had been an affair, but again this was by then evidently terminated, his partner writing that she was heart-broken but agreed he must not break up his family and home. The usual scenes followed. Ignoring the fact that the relationship had already been ended for her and the family's sake, and making no allowance for having herself failed her husband in many ways over the years, my mother now, with the proof of his infidelity in hand, demanded a divorce. She only consented to stay until May to give him time to sort out his business difficulties. However, when matters became worse and the possible liquidation of the firm was men-tioned, she feared she then could not leave at all, as it would look bad that she had put up with her husband's infidelities as long as he was rich but not when he had financial difficulties.

I never knew what caused the breakdown of the business; mother did not men-tion it and perhaps she did not know herself. I only remember old Mademoiselle Lily once mentioning that it was connected with political unrest in the South of Austria (Bosnia and Herzegowina) when the processing plant situated there was destroyed. But I do not know for certain.

In March 1908, father wrote "nothing can be done to prevent the ship sinking", and the family lawyer, Dr Schueller, who meanwhile had become engaged to one of the Taussig daughters, then agreed that divorce was best. My grandmother also took the same view. For a time my mother went to a nursing home on the outskirts of Vienna because of the strain on her nerves, but as she did not improve she went to her parents' house to stay there till the spring weather became more settled; she was then to return to the nursing home. Father tele-phoned but on the advice of the family which, as my mother wrote in her memoirs, coincided with her own wishes, she refused to speak to him. Instead, on April 16th, her sister Anna met father to discuss terms of a divorce and when she returned she said he had spoken of a long journey he was to undertake, but had now agreed to all mother's proposals for divorce, asking only that she should give him a few weeks time for the repayment of her dowry. The same day father took us boys, who had been staying in our own home, to the best toyshop in the City where we were allowed to choose whatever we wanted. He then went with us to the best Patisserie where he met some friends and ordered Easter presents for various lady friends.

At the time of his conversation with my aunt he had already written several goodbye letters, one of them to my mother, all secured with black sealing wax which his valet had been sent out specially to buy. The next morning he was found dead in bed with a bullet wound in his temple.

31

Chapter 3
MY EARLY YOUTH

I did not know anything about this at the time. Everybody realised how attached I had been to my father, and I was at first told he was in hospital with appendicitis, then that he had gone on a journey, and only some weeks later that he had died, the cause of his death being given to me as appendicitis. I still remember vividly how I hid myself in a recess behind a cupboard and shed bitter tears.

It was only much later that I learned from diaries of my mother how he had died. I also realised from them that though comparatively badly off, my father's financial situation would not have been desperate, but for him not being wealthy meant poverty and this he could not face, particularly as he knew he would not find any support from his wife. His goodbye letter to mother read:—

"Dear Clara,

You have refused to say goodbye to me, goodbye for ever, and therefore I say my farewell in writing.

I clear away what is an obstacle to your recovery of health and happiness and I hope this time at last I shall succeed in my purpose.

Educate the children *sensibly*, make them into good men. You yourself Clara beware of rash decisions; you are too impressionable. Always take the advice of your experienced mother, also in questions of education. I gave Dr Schueller all instructions regarding the financial security for the future of you all. I hope he will succeed so that you will be independent and free of worries, and probably also happy. This is my most fervent and sincere wish. Maybe you will in time realise that I was not quite as bad and objectionable as I seem to you now.

Think sometimes of me and with no bitterness, and keep my memory alive in the children."

My mother's reaction, in her notes of those days, was "Now I am free, young, and the two children exclusively my possession."

There is no doubt that when I got to know the circumstances of the marriage and father's death I sided with him, particularly when I read his last letter and realised how it had been disregarded. Mother had mentioned him but rarely, and when she did it was with bitterness, and she certainly did nothing to keep a kind memory of him alive in the sons.

Since then I could offer her only sympathy, gratitude for many sacrifices she made, and filial care, but not the affection she craved. She was right when, many years later, after I had visited her in London she wrote in her diary: "Kary brought eggs — flowers — everything except his heart."

My mother with her two sons in 1908.

During my childhood all that had passed was, of course, unknown to me. Though I missed father for a long time, saddened whenever I remembered I would never see him again, I was used to his absence for long spells during his business trips.

I now know that, to help grandfather Wilhelm, the three sons-in-law bought the block of houses containing the office, his flat and ours. He went on living where he was; everything else, including our former flat, was let, but the family retained the ownership which, after their deaths, was split between their children. One daughter, who had lived in Hungary and whom I had not met for some 55 years though we had continued an occasional correspondence, died widowed, childless and intestate in 1969, and as all the nearest relations were cousins of her or her late husband I strangely became by inheritance the owner of a one-twelfth share of the two houses. Split up between the many heirs (some of them receiving a one-thirty-second share) the houses are unsaleable but, managed by an Agent whom I do not know personally but who assisted the family for many years, they bring me a small rent.

My aunt, Hedwig Spiegler, the youngest of my father's sisters and the only one who lived in Vienna, and her husband became our guardians and contributed to our education. The change in our circumstances made no impression on me, because though now the "poor relations" we still lived comfortably.

33

Our former drawing room with its treasures had to be sold but most of the other things were kept, even the contents of "the cellar" — some 350 bottles. Of course, henceforth we lived in smaller flats and with fewer servants, but every flat — and we moved several times for varied reasons — was pleasant with four or five rooms and in "good districts". Mother still had her maid Lina, who had been in our house since before my birth, and as cook came the hitherto kitchen-maid of the grandparents, therefore no stranger to us. Lina took charge of us whenever mother was out or had visitors, and then we had a good time in the kitchen quarters.

In the first year we lived in Hietzing, one of the districts of Vienna on the fringe of town and country, fashionable because the Emperor's summer palace Schoenbrunn was situated there. Apart from the fresh air, it was the distance from the City which influenced mother's decision because, as during the year of official mourning, she had to be "out of circulation" anyway, she preferred to be far from society life. However, there was no lack of visitors. One young officer who had been in love with her for a long time frequently came to the house and urged mother to marry him. She had at first almost fled into his loving care, but the relationship became less and less happy as time went on. Both families were against the marriage, and mother's emotionalism and moodiness made him write one day: "You have a strange gift to make life difficult for those who love you." When he failed an examination for the Diplomatic Service he hoped to enter, and both families increased their resistance to the marriage, she gradually withdrew. Later she wrote in her memoirs: "I nearly did the most stupid thing: marrying him — I did not love him and was in love only with his love for me."

Other suitors came during this first period, and we boys had a lovely time as each tried to make friends with us. We were taken out to the People's Prater and our presence was claimed when they came for an evening meal, which meant that we could stay up later than usual, and were allowed to have some of the food which did not normally belong to the children's diet. The only woman friend was the wife of father's former friend and doctor, a man mother had always disliked; she avoided seeing him and actually the friendship with his wife only blossomed when she became a widow.

During this first year we were taken fairly often to mother's parents, which I always found boring. After having been asked how I got on with my lessons, we had nothing to talk about. To my father's father we were taken but rarely, usually for Sunday lunch for which we remained without mother. She and her father-in-law had never got on well. I had always to overcome a certain resistance to these visits, as I found the smell of the hides, which still lingered over the old Stores and permeated the house, rather hard to bear. Also, since the death of his wife before I was born, my grandfather's housekeeper was an elderly, hunch-backed spinster — who I now know was very kind but who then frightened me somewhat. She always had lunch with us. In spite of these obstacles grandfather and I got on very well, and I still treasure some letters left from our frequent correspondence. By the way, I was always told that I took more after him than anybody else in the family.

My mother's mother in 1910.   I in 1908.

That summer we spent on the Semmering, a resort equally fashionable in summer and winter, perched about 2,500 feet up on the side of a mountain pass. There were many high-class hotels, and though mother felt more than a little sorry for herself, being no longer able to stay at the largest and most well-known, we were very comfortable. Actually, that stay in some way influenced my later outlook. Lifts always have a fascination for small boys, and that hotel lift had the added attraction of being attended by a little black boy called Daniel. We made friends, and he subsequently came a lot to our rooms to play with me. Then one morning the manager came to ask if any of our belongings were missing; Daniel was just being taken away by the police for stealing from hotel guests. Nothing of ours was missing, although Daniel had easier access to our rooms than anywhere else; it was obvious that he felt we were friends, and one doesn't steal from friends. I highly appreciated this code of honour, and it no doubt contributed significantly to my friendly feelings towards other races.

The following spring — the year of mourning being over — it was decided that mother should move into Town and nearer to the Grammar School my brother was to enter. The summer was spent in Strobl (on the lake of St Wolfgang on which also the famous White Horse Inn is situated). We lived on the top floor of a house the grandparents had rented and there were very nice children of neighbouring summer guests to play with, in particular a little girl called René.

In that autumn, Theodor Taussig was taken ill; there was still a great eve-of-wedding party for one of his daughters at his house (a mansion he had built in Hietzing), but he rapidly deteriorated and died in November, the diagnosis being arsenical poisoning from the green silk wall-covering in his office at the Bank.

At the instigation of his son-in-law and family lawyer, he left my mother an annuity on condition that she was not to marry her first suitor (not knowing that she had already broken with him) and that any marriage should have the consent of two sons-in-law, the lawyer and Dr Wassermann. My mother was offended and furious and wanted to decline the legacy, but our guardian made it clear to her that she could not do so, and her two cousins assured her that their consent was only a formality, they would never withold it, but had not wanted to contradict Theodor Taussig. Incidentally, my mother never remarried.

The summer of 1910 we spent on another of the Austrian lakes, and whilst we had for a long time had teachers for school work during the winter, it was the first time that we had a tutor with us on the summer holidays. It is one of the things for which I shall always feel indebted and grateful to my mother that she realised we should have male company and not grow up among women only. It probably accounts for my never having become intimate friends with any of my contemporaries; these young men — usually University students — who were engaged as tutors for us were so much more interesting to me.

That summer a Captain in the Cavalry was introduced to mother. He was still on active service but on sick leave, suffering from chronic bronchitis and about half as old again as she. He was an inveterate batchelor, but though they saw each other only spasmodically, a friendship developed which lasted until his death in 1937 at the age of 79. We boys had a great time with him that summer: he was full of fun and always encouraged and helped us to play tricks on mother. In particular I remember one day when we rowed out to a little island and pretended to fasten the boat. However, when mother was not looking, we pushed it off shore into the lake having first tied to it a rope which, submerged in the water, could not be seen. "The boat, the boat" we cried, pointing to it floating some distance from the shore. As we had hoped, my mother was in distress. "How shall we get home?" We enjoyed the situation to the full up to the climax, when we proudly hauled the boat back on the rope which we had secured to a tree.

In those next years up to the War we repeatedly moved house though I am not quite sure why. We had one more stay in Hietzing and several in various districts situated more centrally in Vienna. Eventually we settled in a particularly nice flat and as mother had now taken to painting, encouraged by several artist friends, especially the painters Engelhardt and Klimt and the sculptor Hermann Hahn, she had a studio in the neighbouring house. For this studio she had specially made furnishings in Japanese style, with many embroidered old Japanese silk cushions and old Japanese woodcuts on the walls. All these she had chosen with Hahn that summer in Munich, where he lived. We spent several days there on our way to nearby Berchtesgaden where we stayed for the rest of the summer. During the move to this last flat we lost our old maid Lina who had been charged

I about 1912.

with supervising the move into the flat. When mother came one evening to inspect progress she noticed a movement of the wardrobe door and found one of the packers hiding there. Lina had invited him for the evening and, my mother thought, probably for the night, and that was the end of Lina in our house!

A new maid was taken on, besides the cook, but I have no recollection of her. Now, old Mademoiselle Lily — the same who had been in my grandparents' house and already then had become the confidante of my mother — joined the household. Looking back I should think she was meant partly to act as chaperone for mother, partly to supervise us, and probably mother hoped we would learn French. However, I still had teachers as well, as I did not go to school until I reached grammar school age, but meanwhile, at the end of every year, had to sit a public examination. My brother, who was already in grammar school, did not last long there. When he had failed one year's form examinations and mother received a very bad report about his behaviour, there were violent scenes between her and him at home. Consequently he was sent to a school outside Vienna, living with one of the masters. Boarding schools were not usual in Austria, there were only one or two for the sons of officers serving abroad, the others were for "naughty boys" and had not a good reputation: the usual solution for boys like my brother was, therefore, the one my mother chose.

Among my teachers then was one for English which I had again almost forgotten, and later also a French teacher, as my mother realised that though she and Mademoiselle usually conversed in French, I improved Mademoiselle's German but not she my French.

Mademoiselle Lily had no great educational influence on me but she "mothered" me and we got on very well. As she had already shown when my mother was a girl, she had in typical French ways a great understanding of love. I

37

was then about 11, had fallen deeply in love with a dancing-school partner aged 8, and was longing to have a lock of her hair. Mademoiselle Lily was very ready to help, and one day when we were at the ice-rink she said to the little girl "Come Louise I must adjust your bonnet which isn't straight" and, with scissors she had hidden, quickly cut off a little lock. I carried that curl for many years in a locket on a thin chain round my neck.

In 1913 my father's father died, and in the same summer my mother's father had his 70th birthday which, in the old tradition, was celebrated with a play written jointly by all the children in which they and the grandchildren acted. I remember two things about the play: I played cupid and there is still a photograph in my possession which shows me in my costume of pink silk, armed with a gold bow and arrow. I also recall the beginning of the play, with mother's sister receiving a letter, looking at it and saying: "A registered letter and over-stamped — that can only be from Clara", a very appropriate pointer to my mother's proverbial extravagance.

The next summer, 1914, saw us again in the neighbourhood of Munich, actually on the Schliersee. All I remember from our stay there is that we were a very happy party of summer guests, all of us musical, and in the evenings we formed a small band of zither and guitar players singing lustily. I myself played the guitar, and still had a very good soprano voice.

The pleasure was short-lived. The Austrian heir to the throne was assassinated, and this was followed, on July 29th, by a declaration of war on Serbia, and soon also by Germany and Russia. Then France and England joined the war on the other side.

During mobilisation one could not travel, and when it again became possible the journey home — which would normally have taken something like four hours — took thirty. Mademoiselle Lily and our tutor were with us. The only other thing I remember about the journey was that we had to change trains in Salzburg, stepping carefully over the soldiers who were asleep on the platforms. We eventually arrived in Vienna to be greeted by the news that grandmother was to be operated on for cancer. Consequently we moved into the grandparents' flat, still with Mademoiselle Lily and mother's maid; there was room for us as my younger uncle — who had lately lived in Paris — had been interned in France, and his older brother had joined up. Before he left, he had married his girl friend of many years standing; she was a Christian and did not belong to their society, but with the war on, his parents had not the heart to object. This aunt was a charming person, became a great favourite of mine, and was a blessing to my uncle, standing by him faithfully when, many years later, Hitler came to power, and many "Aryan" wives left their husbands.

My brother remained with the schoolmaster; I continued in grammar school which I had entered about two years previously and where I did very well. Having witnessed my brother being asked all day long whether he had done his school work, and loving my peace and quiet, I decided to avoid the same fate. My then tutor, Franz Weiss, I liked very much indeed, and he probably influenced my life much more than I realised at the time. A Catholic law student, he never mentioned religion as such, but his whole personality made a great impression on me. He stayed with me through all my time in grammar school, except for one year when he had to sit his law examinations. He later became the equivalent of the permanent Under-Secretary in the Ministry of Agriculture and a great friend of mine. I also became his doctor.

In Vienna the heads of the various Ministries were automatically offered free of charge boxes at the Opera and the State Theatre; the equivalent of the Foreign Office and the Home Office received them every night, the smaller Ministries two or three times a week. When the Minister did not use the box he would hand the entitlement on to his permanent Under-Secretary, and in the case of the Minister of Agriculture — when the Under-Secretary could not use it — he offered the box to his doctor! Hence I had a lovely time going frequently to the Opera and the State Theatre, inviting my friends in style which, of course, brought me some return invitations.

During the one year in which I did not have my usual tutor, his place was taken by a person of a rather different type. A Theosophist, tee-totaller and vegetarian, a great idealist but one whose philosophy did not appeal to me at all. I never really became attached to the man but feel now that I owe him a good deal, because it was in conversation with him that I developed a fair argumentative power which in later years stood me in good stead.

School days were very hum-drum, consisting of lessons and homework; recreation was not considered to be of concern to the school. Matters became worse when, after the outbreak of War, my school, which was a large and rather stately building, was converted into a hospital and we were transferred to another school building which we had to share. It meant lessons on three mornings and three afternoons a week, the other school occupying the buildings on the other half days. The shorter school hours (no more full days) meant more homework, and in the later years some pre-military training was fitted in. After all we were to be the age-group next on the call-up list if the War had lasted any longer. I reached the rank of Patrol Leader and got fairly proficient in map-reading and shooting which latter, however, I did only in the position of lying prone on the ground as otherwise the rifle was too heavy for me. On the whole the years of the First World War have in my memory shrunk into a few basic pictures: the family sitting and knitting "comforts for the troops" and worrying about my uncle who, serving with the field guns, seems to have been always in the front line. But he returned uninjured except for considerable deafness which was ascribed to the continuous gunfire with which he had to live. For some particularly brave act he got a very high decoration which, later on, helped him to survive the Hitler period.

My brother too had joined up, volunteering at the age of 17, and we all felt it was not so much because of enthusiasm for the War as to escape school. He served in the Cavalry and I remember my mother buying a horse for him. He never reached the front, and is the only case I know of an officer-cadet returning on leave to take his matric and failing it. During the few weeks' school attendance which were prescribed and for which leave was granted, he never tried to study, but attended school in uniform, with jingling spurs, to the annoyance of the teachers. He is also the only case I know of who successfully pressed his mother to buy him a dress uniform during the War. I do not think he had ever any opportunity to wear it except for school attendance! However, the brown uniform coat, then dyed black, served me after the War for many years as a winter overcoat.

One summer early in the War stays particularly in my memory. It was shortly before my Uncle Otto joined the Army. I stayed with him and my favourite Aunt Emmy in a little village; the summer guests got together to act a play for some charitable cause, and the Committee celebrated with a meal afterwards. Not knowing anything about drink I thought it was a good idea to empty what was left in the glasses after the guests had got up from the table, and thus drank a fair amount of mixed alcohol, with somewhat disastrous results. At first I drew the attention of my uncle to myself by chasing the girls, and he took me outside the inn to ask whether I saw one church tower or two. I decided on one. He next asked me whether I saw one moon or two, which I found much more difficult, probably because by then the drink had taken a greater hold on me. Still I decided on one. "Then you can stay and carry on" he said. The evening ended for me when I fell off the raised dance platform, slinking home to nurse my cut nose. I still bear the scar!

The highlight of the summer for me was the presence of my aunt's youngest sister, I guess then about 18 years old. I thought I had fallen in love with her, and in typical Austrian fashion went after dark serenading in front of her window ("fensterln"). We then talked a little and in the end she said, I thought tenderly, "Now go home", putting her arm through the bars of the window and stroking my face. When I arrived home I found my forehead and cheeks streaked with black — she had evidently dipped a cork in soot and stroked me with that and, pretending to be tender, made me look ridiculous for my foolishness. But I did not bear her any grudge and we remained friends, exchanging letters even now.

But in the main my recollections of the War are of the terribly dry maize bread which was all we could obtain in later years. With the little and not very good margarine allowed on ration, it was difficult to swallow and even the meagre spread of fruit preserve available did not help much. Now and again this hardship was relieved by a friend of my mother's, who was a high officer and owned a large country estate, sending his batman with a rucksack full of fresh country provisions, which made for a few feast days.

Into the War years fell the death of our Emperor, Francis Joseph, who had reigned 1848 to 1916, longer even than Queen Victoria. We watched his funeral from a window in the flat of my Aunt Sidonie, the widow of Uncle Theodor. We all felt it was the end of an era, and so it was. When the War ended the Austrian-Hungarian Empire broke up, and life appeared very miserable. My uncle returned from the War and gradually rebuilt his solicitor's practice. My brother left the

I with my tutor in 1920.

Army which, now that the glamour of an Imperial Army had gone, had no more attraction for him and, through friends, my mother managed to get him a job as a clerk in a dairy. I continued with grammar school, and in spring 1920, managed to pass my matric with distinction.

Since my grandmother's death, we had in the last part of the War once again moved into the grandparents' flat to look after grandfather who, by that time, had become something of an invalid with hardening of the arteries. This often led to spells of confusion, mainly at night, and I remember him several times jumping out of bed in fright saying that lions were prowling around. He had a resident nurse to look after him, but when she had her day off my mother and I shared the nursing duties, which consisted largely of keeping him company while he played Patience by the hour. I don't know exactly when he died but it was certainly before I left grammar school. My mother then took over the flat completely, and her younger brother Fredi, having being released from internment in France, joined us, occupying the two rooms which formerly were grandfather's. As a professional painter, he used one room as a studio; I rarely saw him paint but he was usually stretched out on a couch waiting for inspiration.

My brother stayed with us for a few months but — after some scenes with mother — found his own bed-sitter.

Chapter 4
MEDICAL STUDENT

When I had passed my matric I unhesitatingly decided on a medical career. I had always considered doctor's work as a special vocation, but there were also some practical considerations. The subjects at which I was best in school were Physics and Greek, which are usually not supposed to go together. However, Mathematics was my worst subject and I knew that I could not get very far as a physicist without Mathematics. What had appealed to me was practical, experimental Physics and actually, since my early years in grammar school, I spent hours with my Physics Master in the school laboratory. At home I often demonstrated physical experiments, accompanied by lecturing, which made me feel very grand; as a matter of fact, these were probably the first signs of my instructional abilities which I later put to good use. In Greek I read Plato for my pleasure, and the study of Philosophy appealed to me, but I had no real gift for languages; other subjects classed as art, like History or Art itself, did not appeal to me at all. Medicine seemed to me the obvious choice as a field in which Science and Art meet. When I told our family doctor of my plans he said encouragingly: "You will be all right as long as you don't treat your patients like you treat yourself." And so I entered University as a medical student. Being born at the end of December I was, at the start of term, not quite 18.

The two-and-a-half years of pre-clinical studies seemed to me not very much different from school, except for the practical part of anatomy which meant dissecting dead bodies. I had been warned by well-meaning friends and relations that I would probably be too sensitive for this, but from the first I did not find it off-putting or even strange. Dead bodies had never frightened me, and in this particular setting my interest was absorbed to such an extent that I almost forgot that the body once belonged to a human being like me. Physics and Chemistry were much the same as we had been taught in school. Biology too was just like another school subject, and actually of less interest to me than Logic and Psychology which had been taught in the top form. I was, therefore, rather pleased when it was replaced in our time-table by Physiology and Histology which involved practical exercises.

The lectures left plenty of spare time. I had never before made close friendships with contemporaries nor did I do so now, and as I did not care for drinking or smoking, I never joined a Students' Association. However, through a friend, the son of my father's former doctor, who was a few years older than I, and at that time the Committee Chairman of the Annual Medical Students' Ball, I was invited to join that Committee and accepted. The Ball was a great success which the Committee afterwards celebrated in the Chairman's house with a bottle party. There was a plot that I, as the youngest member, should be "drunk under

Our old Viennese family doctor.

the table". I knew when I had had enough, and pleaded that I did not want any more drink, however, the custom on the Continent required that whenever one's health was drunk you clinked glasses and drank. This custom was insisted upon, and one after the other the Committee members drank my health. The inevitable happened. I was later told that my last words before falling asleep were that my mother should be informed that I would not return home until morning. When, on waking next morning, I found myself lying on the couch in the doctor's examination room, a pail tied round my neck, and with a splitting headache, I promised myself never again to drink more than I wanted and knew I could take, even if it meant giving offence. This resolution I have kept.

Most of my leisure time was spent at home reading. My mother, who had always been a society lady, was rather taken aback by this, and often told me that she had never known anybody as old as me! All the same, it was in those years that my mother and I were closer to each other than at any other time before or after.

I do not know how it was done, as I was told that through investing money in War Loan we had now, for the second time, lost what wealth was left — or had been recovered by old shares gaining in value — but there always seemed to be money for holidays. One I particularly remember. We stayed for three weeks in a hotel on the sea front in Brioni, and then went on to Venice. The hotel in Brioni — later the headquarters of Tito and consequently closed — was very luxurious. All day was spent on the beach, and for lunch the guests came in their beach attire, but in the evenings the men wore dinner jackets, the ladies summer evening dresses, and there was dancing after dinner. My interest was completely taken up by a couple; he, an obviously very prosperous, typical German, business man, was but a foil for her — a much younger woman of a strange and fascinating beauty, probably Dalmatian. In the three weeks we stayed at the hotel I never saw her wear the same beach wear or evening dress more than once, and each evening I waited with bated breath to see her and to see what she was wearing.

My mother applauded my interest as I had never before shown any in girls, and she hoped that this would be the moment to awaken me to them. Actually, she was quite wrong. I was always interested in girls and in their ways, and whenever I joined a dancing lesson or a party, I quickly paired up. I admired them, their femininity and intuition, and I knew I needed them as a complement to my own male attitude. I could talk for hours to girls, but they were not objects of sexual interest or greed to me, they were interesting companions.

Sex appeared to me as something that should necessarily be bound up with love, and to love one had to have a long-lasting connection with joint interests as in marriage, when the common desire to build up a home, a family and a future would be a close tie. If work together was possible as well, this would be the perfection of all dreams. Already then I saw the sexes as equal, but I never believed that they should compete in doing the same. The woman was to be the help-mate of the man, but though I then had never heard it so formulated I felt that behind every successful man there must be the right woman. What I believed then — and still believe — was recently expressed by the actress Penelope Keith in one of her television programmes: "I don't believe in the equality of the sexes; what was wrong when we were the dominant part?"

Anyway, the clothes of the beautiful stranger filled my thoughts and were a steady source of comment and conversation between mother and myself, but as soon as we had left, the episode was over, and my thoughts became completely absorbed by Venice. It was the first time I had seen that City, then still much cleaner with less mechanical traffic and more beautiful than in later years, when on several subsequent visits its decay saddened me. Moreover, we arrived by boat, having the first view of Venice from the sea on to the Piazetta, the Palace of the Doges and St Mark's Cathedral, an unforgettable impression.

Of other summers I remember walks with my mother, talking with her about life and God, in whom she strongly believed, but who for her was just some magical, impersonal force, ubiquitous, who should be approached and adored in the open country rather than in church. From her I was imbued with some such Pantheistic ideas which I held for many years, leading me to ridicule, in my mind, and sometimes in conversation, the idea of an almighty personal God. "If he is almighty can he create a stone so heavy that he cannot lift it?" was one of my arguments. Much later I recognised the absurdity and futility of such arguments.

Part of another summer was spent in the 17th century manor which a relation had bought in Styria. His wife was a cousin of my late father, he himself a soap manufacturer who had made a fortune and now saw himself as a squire with manor, gardens, woods and a hunt. His carriage was drawn by a pair of grey horses of the famous Lipizzan breed which he had bought from the old Imperial stables. Our hosts were very amiable, though he himself was somewhat peculiar, having a phobia about germs, appropriate I thought for a soap manufacturer! He never touched a door handle without gloves but usually a servant was at hand to open the door for him. It was all very splendid but not really ostentatious. To me the best part was the company of his daughter, a very pretty girl, slightly older than myself. We became great friends, had a lot to talk about, but the idea of love or sex never entered my head. Every evening we danced to gramophone music while the various members of the large house party sat around playing bridge. They were all contemporaries of the parents, considered old by us, though they were very much younger than I am now as I write this. Occasionally they looked up from their playing cards, glancing and nodding approvingly. I am sure they exchanged comments like "Aren't they sweet?", but I could not have cared less what they thought or said. My interest was in the dancing, and Mitzi — a perfect partner. Because I cared for style, I enquired every teatime what she would be wearing in the evening, and then we went together to the greenhouses to choose for me a buttonhole matching the colour of her dress.

My brother and my uncle, who lived with us, both of them womanisers at that time, evidently shared my mother's concern that it was unnatural for a young man — and a medical student at that — not to have any manly desires. Consequently they invited me one evening to visit a brothel with them — they were legal in Vienna in those days. We entered the very plush reception hall and dance room, and a lot of girls in their underwear, supposed to be alluring, crowded round us encouragingly. I took one look and found the scene revolting. "Have a good evening," I said to my two escorts, "I am going home" — and I did.

Then one day my mother took on a new maid, blonde with big blue eyes. "Ah," the three of us said with one voice when she had left the room after serving the evening meal. "She is much too good for your ideas," mother replied sternly. But she was not. She became the first "adventure" of my life, but we had little to say to each other, and I soon became disenchanted. I then heard that she had also become very friendly with both my brother and my uncle, and that confirmed my original idea that without genuine emotion there was nothing to a sexual relationship.

The first two-and-a-half years completed, and the examinations in the preclinical disciplines behind me, I now entered the clinical years. I do not know how they are organised in Vienna now, but then they consisted mainly of lectures with little opportunity for practical work. Consequently, the freshly qualified doctor was not really expected to be competent to practice his profession before he had gone through a post-graduate training and this was indeed the strength of the Vienna Medical School. To become a specialist no particular examinations were required, but appointments of a specified kind had to be held for a certain length of time at particular hospitals; only then could one apply for a consultant's job. The specifications were different for various disciplines. Regarding general practice, even though there was no legal bar, no self-respecting young doctor would enter it without prolonged post-graduate training, usually serving a rotating internship of altogether four years, being allocated twice to each department in the hospital, once as a junior and then as a senior houseman. Completion of the internship gave the doctor the right to describe himself as "emerited" from his hospital and to put this fact on the plate showing his consulting hours.

Many of our University teachers were of international fame. The surgeons were von Eiselsberg, the principal pupil of his predecessor the world famous Billroth, and Hochenegg who made his name designing an operation for rectal carcinoma. Among the physicians who held Chairs in medicine, Wenckebach was outstanding. A Dutchman by birth, he spent years in general practice but then specialised in heart diseases, and pioneered the work on heart rhythms and electrocardiography. The instrument in those days took up a whole room with innumerable wires: today some are portable instruments of attache-case size. Neurology and Psychiatry were taught by Wagner-Jauregg, a Nobel prize winner. However, much that was offered in the lectures could be learned from books, and thus I decided to reduce my attendance at them, concentrating mainly on practical exercises which were usually led by an assistant (a grade half-way between senior registrar and junior consultant) except for laryngology where Professor Hayek was always present himself. He was effectively the founder of modern laryngology, well known all over the world, and particularly in this country. I remember one of our local consultant laryngologists remarking one day that general practitioners did not use forehead mirrors any longer, to which I replied: "Of course I do, my teacher, Hayek, would turn in his grave if I did not." "Hayek?", he queried, "not THE Hayek?" But it was THE Hayek. From then on the consultant paid me special attention.

Instead of attending lectures which I did not consider to be of importance, I decided to lay a solid foundation to my later clinical work by working as a volunteer in the Pathological Department of one of our large State hospitals under Professor Stoerk, an eminent pathologist. I asked for an interview and explained to him that I was thinking of surgery as a career and that I would like to work in pathology as a preliminary to it. Professor Stoerk willingly accepted me and advised that I should start my training with the basic technicalities, because if, later on, I had to supervise laboratory assistants I would have to know their job myself and be able to demonstrate to them what I wanted done and how. Consequently, I learnt from each technician, starting with the wrapping and sterilising of glassware, how to prepare the nutrition media for microbe cultures, how to make the glass pipettes which we used to add drops of different fluids to various media, and eventually I graduated to the preparation of specimens for histological examination. My teacher in this was Professor Stoerk's senior laboratory assistant, the most famed in all Vienna, to whom all the

46

important scholars went to have their microscopical slides prepared if they intended to use them as illustrations in their scientific publications. Under his guidance I soon became proficient in this field. At the same time I watched post-mortem examinations, which were conducted by the Chief or one of his two assistants; the number of post-mortems in the department being more than 1,200 a year. In time I graduated to doing histological and pathological examinations and post-mortem examinations myself, first under supervision, but after about a year I was entrusted to do them on my own for the various hospital departments. This, according to a testimonial by the senior assistant given to me after the death of Professor Stoerk, was "a rare exception and a sign of particular recognition and complete confidence" on the part of the Chief.

However, not to lose contact with clinical medicine, I worked simultaneously part-time in various clinical departments, which I was allowed to do as all the departmental heads knew me well from the post-mortem examinations which I had conducted for them. In a comparatively short time — a few months in each department — I thus learned much more of clinical medicine than I could have done from lectures, thereby laying a good foundation for my examinations as well as for my medical future.

After about one-and-a-half years, at the wish of Professor Stoerk, I transferred my activities mainly to the University Institute of Pathological Histology and Bacteriology of which he was also the head. But I still kept in touch with the hospital's pathological department.

Professor Stoerk attended the University Institute mainly in the late afternoon and evening — during the day the effective head was his assistant, himself a university lecturer and head of the pathological departments at two small private hospitals. He usually went home soon after the chief had arrived, and in fact I therefore acted as assistant to them both, to the one during the day, and the other until late in the evening. Soon I myself became involved in research work. With the consent of Professor Stoerk I transformed the otherwise little-used library room into one of my own, and often stayed in the laboratory until late at night, occasionally even sleeping on a camp bed when I wanted to check on the progress of some experiment. At intervals, between inspections, I studied my examination subjects, but by then — fascinated by that work — I had in my own mind decided to give up the idea of becoming a surgeon and to remain a pathologist.

The job of demonstrator at the Institute became vacant, and Professor Stoerk sent for me and told me that I had been considered for the appointment, but was still too young; he would, therefore, appoint a young doctor who had been recommended to him, but wanted me to know the reason why I had not been chosen. I had never thought I would be since I was still a student. However, only a few months later, the chief sent for me again, and said he found that the man he had appointed was unsuitable, that he would not keep him on, and would appoint me as demonstrator. "But don't tell the students you have not yet sat your own examination in pathology," he added. Thus, on April 1st, 1924, I became demonstrator with pay which was hardly cigarette money, but made me officially a university employee. The future looked bright, and I loved my job.

The evenings in the laboratory had a magic of their own, and in later years — when I read the life story of an American doctor who also was a demonstrator in pathology (I believe it was "Martin Arrowsmith" by Sinclair Lewis) — I found the same atmosphere described there. Normally I was addressed by my surname, but when strangers were present I was addressed as "doctor" (though, of course, I was still a student). Very occasionally, when we were alone in the laboratory, the chief called me by my first name.

Social life did not mean much to me at that time, but there were so many "inherited" connections between my family and contemporaries that I could not avoid it. Anyway, I loved dancing, and often attended parties after work. Late one evening I remember I was in the laboratory in my dinner jacket to finish a job for the boss. It was not quite up to my usual standard, and I complained about the instrument (the so-called microtome) which was not very good. "My dear boy," Stoerk said, "a good fiddler plays well on a bad fiddle." I always remembered those words, and never again tried to blame an instrument.

It was the time of the so-called "naughty twenties" and there were a lot of house parties, and a very dimly lit room belonged to the fashion of the day. Parents were expected to keep a low profile and kissing and petting went on. I did not care for that, but would rather talk to a pretty girl of my choice until the early hours of the morning. And I danced a lot, a good deal of the thrill being to hold a pretty girl in my arms, to lead her and have her follow my steps; however, the idea of any sexual contact did not even occur to me, much in contrast to the present day when there is plenty of touching between the sexes but in dancing each partner seems to do his own thing.

However, I was certainly not without feeling for the other sex and, quite naturally for those days, I looked for a partner among the "sweet girls of the suburbs". There, according to Arthur Schnitzler the poet, novelist and playwright, whose writings at that time deeply influenced — as a matter of fact almost dictated — the behaviour of the young men of the middle classes, "the first kiss is given with a smile and the parting is without agony — just with tender nostalgia".

For the supply of those girls I had a ready source: my artist uncle, who lived at one end of our flat but with his own front door from the time before the two flats were made into one, or rather his girl friend. She brought young friends to his rooms for me to meet. Some of them were just cheerful company for an evening party, some were status symbols. I particularly remember a beautiful, tall slim girl — a model at a fashion house. She would not go out with me in the evenings for fear of being seen by her "sugar daddy" friend. However, her employer sent her, in model clothes, to the races and she was supposed to be partnered by an elegant young man at the firm's expense. My scene! It was the only occasion on which I went to the races, but I did not watch the horses; I only had eyes for the blonde girl at my side, who looked lovely in a white lace dress and a wide-brimmed hat with a dark velvet ribbon — just right for the front cover of a glossy magazine.

48

At last I found a steady partner — an innocent girl of 16, very pretty — very sweet natured, ideal for outings on Sunday afternoons to the Vienna woods, and evenings in the People's Prater, and for a little evening meal within my means. I met her parents, who were good-hearted, simple people who accepted me as the girl's boy friend though, in the beginning, they evidently did not realise the full implications.

My mother was delighted that I had at last a real girl friend, and as a Christmas present gave me the money to take Lily for Easter on a week's holiday to Salzburg, a place I loved and where I had often been before on my own. The girl's parents were hesitant to let her go with me, realising at last what it would mean. However, I took my courage in both hands and told them that their scruples came too late.

I booked two rooms for "my cousin and myself" and the chambermaid needed little persuasion to unlock the door between the two rooms. I felt very happy, thinking that I would now show Lily the beauty of Salzburg, be her guide, and broaden her view of life. We went out for a walk, crossing the bridge over the dividing stream from the new into the old town, a particularly beautiful scene. "Oh, look at that dog," she said enthusiastically, and my dream was at an end. I tried to behave for the rest of the holiday as a boy friend should, supplying whipped cream and anything else Lily could and did expect, but my heart had gone out of the affair. When, after our return to Vienna, Lily had some silly argument with her parents (nothing to do with me), and put her head into a gas oven, the parents in their distress called for me. I took the girl to a hospital where I had friends, insisting that she should be kept on a general ward to see real hardship, misfortune and misery. When she had recovered, I took her back into the care of her parents, explaining that any further responsibility was beyond me; if a simple row with her parents was sufficient to give her the idea of suicide, what would she do if we eventually parted as was sure to happen one day?

I am now not proud of that episode in my life, but then I had no religious beliefs to influence me. Moreover, as I have said, the spirit of Schnitzler was then the fashion and my mother's lifelong admiration of him had probably penetrated into me to a considerable extent. Thus these "sweet girls of the suburbs" were seen as fair game, born to give love and emotional satisfaction to young men like me. If, in return, we gave the girl some colourful memory to retain when eventually she would settle down to what we were certain would be a hum-drum existence and marriage to a man of her own circle, we felt we had done our share. Even so, I was somewhat uneasy that I had been unfaithful to my own ideals.

It was about that time that my friend, Ernst Hellman, a few years younger than me, the brother of one of our dancing partners, asked my advice on a problem of the heart. For years he had been in love with a young girl, but lately had fallen in love with her best friend and neighbour. When he told the first girl about it, she was so understanding and "behaved so marvellously" that he had again fallen in love with her; now he felt he was in love with two girls and did not know which was the right one. Could I advise? I had no hesitation: the second girl, of course. A love resumed because of some special feature of character was admiration and might strengthen the bonds of friendship, but it was not real love. Of course I was curious to meet the two girls and Ernst told me there would be an early opportunity as his parents were about to arrange a dance for his sister. It was on March 21st, 1925 that I found out how wise my counsel had been. Ernst later married Annemarie, the girl I had "recommended", and it was an excellent marriage which ended only when he died after nearly 52 years. He had graduated in agriculture and managed a farm in Austria, and then became a chicken farmer in Australia whereto they had emigrated after the take-over of Austria by Hitler. And the first girl? I married her and that is now over 54 years ago.

Much later I was told that Magda (short for Magdalena) and I were very unpopular at the party because we sat together near the buffet. We had neither eyes nor ears for anything nor anybody, but even so, it seems many guests went hungry rather than disturb us. We sat and talked, and though we took part in the dances we returned quickly to our chairs still talking. Magda was not quite 16 then but I was certain she was right for me.

When the party ended we had arranged to meet again soon, and Ernst agreed he would take me on his motor cycle. He came to collect me a few days later and we set off with me on the pillion seat, but less than half way there he collided with a handcart; I received no serious injury but dirty, bleeding and with torn trousers was deposited back home, while Ernst went to give the sad news that the rendezvous had to be cancelled. Sad for me and Magda — as far as Ernst was concerned I always suspected that the accident was a Freudian slip on his part. Anyway, he was not keen on making another early attempt to take me, persuaded me that Magda was too young for me, and eventually I gave in and wrote to her. I do not know exactly what I said in my letter but I still have her reply. "I just want to tell you that I fully understand and though I am *terribly* sad I realise that you are right. To meet just once more would not have been much good and for me at least it would have made matters even more difficult. To really be something to you I am unfortunately still too young and I am quite aware that I could not possibly satisfy you yet. I certainly will not forget you and hope that you too will keep a good memory of me. Just one thing I would still ask you — please let me keep your letter. Nobody will find it, of that you can be certain. If, however, you insist on having it returned I shall send it by Ernst."

I now more than ever concentrated on work. It was understood that the demonstrator not only assisted the students but also trained prospective laboratory assistants. I remember two such pupils. One about twelve years my senior went later to Rochester, New York, and there became one of the top technical assistants in the hospital's blood laboratory. She is now 91 and, of course, has long since retired, but is obviously still an active woman in house and garden and even drives a car. We write to each other every Christmas.

The other was a girl a little younger than myself, daughter of a Jewish jeweller, with the typical southern beauty of the Sephardim Jews. She intended to make a

My schoolgirl-wife at the time we first met.

career as a laboratory assistant. We became great friends and I often had an evening meal in her house among her family. Her sister was a follower of Rudolf Steiner which led to long discussions. Helen herself had no particular religious affiliation but believed in God, was kind, quiet and serious. Common interest was a strong bond, and in my then state of feeling lost and lonely I grew very fond of her, a feeling she seemed to reciprocate with gentleness and tender care. However, there was an atmosphere of melancholy, almost gloom, in her bearing as if she carried the whole burden of Jewish suffering on her shoulders. There was no sense of humour, no laughter, and I soon recognised that common work and common interests are not enough to form a lasting bond — there must be that mysterious "click", undefinable, but well known the world over as love. We talked about our feelings in a sensible, nostalgic way and drifted apart.

In the lab, where I was demonstrator at the time I met my wife.

Work again occupied my mind — but not fully. There was still the vision of Magda, fresh and eager, partly still beautiful child, but already with the promise of lovely womanhood. I made up my mind and prevailed on Ernst to let us meet again. Eventually he arranged it, and I waited for her near the school when she went home. She lived on the outskirts of Vienna, where town and country met, in the wine district known as Grinzing, in a modern family house built by one of the fashionable architects. We took a way through the vineyards, and it was the first of many such walks. There were other opportunities to meet her when she managed to get out on her own. Little letters went to and fro, making appointments, and Annemarie was most helpful in giving me the freedom of her address for my letters to Magda. Among the letters I still possess is one in which Magda wrote: "If you have really nothing better to do (work must come first) wait for me at 3 o'clock on the corner where we met last time. I shall try to get out on my own but I cannot promise. If I am not alone you must disappear. If you cannot manage to come I shall certainly not be cross with you — I stand in such awe of your work."

I could often arrange to meet Magda in the afternoon and then make up for it by working late in the evening, because I was then also deeply involved in the reasearch work Professor Stoerk had advised me to undertake. It concerned a theory — which he thought was rather far-fetched — about some heart murmurs put forward by one of the professors holding a chair in medicine at the university. I was able to disprove its supposed anatomical basis and demonstrated the results of my research to the Association of Viennese Pathologists the very evening before I sat my examination in that subject. Later that year my paper appeared

52

My wife as a child aged about 4 years.   My wife as a child about 10 years old.

in print in the leading pathological journal and, introduced by Professor Stoerk, I presented a copy personally to Professor Wenckebach. He was very kind, said he had never believed the theory of his colleague, and was delighted.

The long summer vacation, which left me free at the University Institute, I spent at a small country hospital. The superintendent was a friend of my Uncle Otto and, at his request, willingly accepted me as a temporary volunteer. The medical staff consisted of the superintendent (a consultant surgeon) and two assistants who had also considerable experience in general medicine. The two were great friends, but hardly ever able to go out together because one or other had to be on duty. They made me most welcome, saying: "At last we have somebody we can leave in charge of the routine work." They left me their telephone number to call them if I was in difficulty, but on the whole they thought I would be able to cope with the assistance of (really under the guidance of) the theatre sister who was a wise and experienced old nun. We did cope. The work was very varied. Much casualty work, particularly agricultural injuries, some medical emergencies and, mainly on Saturday evenings, drunken men coming in, sometimes vagrants in search of a bed, sometimes maudlin husbands suddenly wanting to visit a sick wife. Having my work afterwards checked by one of the doctors I learned a lot in those two months, and my experience with the drunks still stands me in good stead in my work as a police surgeon.

Soon after the summer holidays I was introduced to Magda's parents, Egon and Emmy Wellesz. He was a famous musicologist and composer and, in spite of being a university professor of the history of music, was of a typical easy-going artistic temperament. His wife, herself a well known art historian, was a much sterner type. Even so, it was as early as October 1925, that Magda, in one of her

My wife's father.

My wife's mother.

letters, mentioned that I had found favour in the eyes of her mother who, however, had advised her not to fall in love. Her warning came too late.

I did not see much of my mother during that period. For some time I had been home very little, and she, after many years, met Schnitzler again, and a great friendship developed which made her in time his steady companion. She then moved to an hotel, having let our flat with the stipulation that I would be able to keep my room and have breakfast supplied by our tenants. My brother had left home some time before, after a particularly big scene with mother, when the blonde young maid named him as the father of the child she was expecting. Ostensibly mother had left the flat because she had a financially favourable offer, but I myself always thought it was to have more freedom and to be able to travel with Arthur Schnitzler, which she often did. When she was in Vienna I visited her when I could.

That winter I spent many Sunday afternoons in Magda's house, usually with Ernst and Annemarie, but I worked no less. As a matter of fact I had now to cope with my final examinations as well as with my work as demonstrator. My contacts with the various university departments helped, as I was offered the opportunity of doing ward rounds, and in this way got a kind of crammer course from the assistants in the various departments with whom my work had brought me in touch and I had made friends. I remember particularly my attendance in the university clinics for psychiatry and for eye diseases. Ophthalmology was a much feared subject, and in my case it was the last of the six examinations constituting the finals for the Vienna M.D. I still can almost hear the examiner say: "Isn't it lucky if the other candidates know nothing of the subject — the one who knows a little stands out favourably." It was by no means a brilliant achievement but I was the only candidate who passed that day. A few days later, in full evening dress, as was the custom in Vienna at that time, I became a doctor.

Chapter 5
THE YOUNG DOCTOR

I am sure that, for some time, Magda's parents had become apprehensive, and that it was not only as a finishing school, but also to take her thoughts off me that it had been arranged to send her to a girls' summer school in Switzerland that summer (1926). If I am right that this was the plan, it misfired and achieved the opposite result. We had decided for some time that one day we would be man and wife, and now — just before leaving for Switzerland — she told her father, adding that I wanted to talk to him. "Good heavens that makes me an old man," was his reply — he was then 40! I then wrote to Egon asking for an interview, which he gave me on neutral ground in one of the Viennese coffee houses. "Magda is much too young. Let us wait and see," he said, but he sounded benevolent. I fully agreed that Magda was still too young, she would have to finish school first, but I thought that meantime I should have access to her house more freely without her mother asking before each weekend: "What are you doing this weekend?" — and when told I was coming, trying to make other suggestions. "Those things you must discuss with my wife," Egon replied. "I have always left everything disagreeable to her."

I was young and brave, and faced the mother. "Wait and see," was again the conclusion, though we had a different timing in mind. We both agreed that Magda must first finish school but Emmy wanted her daughter to do a year of household training afterwards, while I thought the best way for that was by practising it as a housewife. Anyway, I gained the concession that the head of the school in Switzerland would be informed of my existence and that Magda was allowed by her parents to write and to receive letters without having them censored. I was, moreover, invited for the end of the summer to Altaussee where the family used to rent a summer villa every year, and where Magda was to join them at the end of her stay in Switzerland. I suppose this was meant as an opportunity for the parents to get to know me better before they made up their minds about me as a prospective member of the family, and I gather I passed their test. Anyway, we were happy during this period.

I, and I suppose most other people, had taken it for granted that my career under Professor Stoerk would be safe, but he was unexpectedly taken ill and died. Our University Institute was subsequently affiliated to the Institute for Pathological Anatomy, and although he confirmed me as a demonstrator, its chief very fairly told me that he would give his old pupils preference in promotion to assistant, which was a basic precondition for an academic career. What now? I wanted to get married as soon as possible and for this I had to offer security. A suitable job was offering itself.

My wife in the Swiss "finishing school"
(unofficially engaged).

My mother shortly before I got married.

Among the private diagnostic laboratories in Vienna was a rather unusual one. It was headed jointly by a university professor for bacteriology and an analytical chemist. Besides the usual diagnostic facilities it contained the largest collection of microbiological cultures which were asked for and sent all over the world, some highly dangerous for scientific purposes, others for industrial use like the yeasts of all kinds of wine. Professor Pribram had received a call to a chair in the United States, which he did not hold at the Vienna University. He accepted, but at the time was not certain whether his stay would be permanent, and he looked for an assistant who could take over his bacteriological work including the maintenance of the collection, which meant permanent supervision and transference of cultures to new media whenever necessary. Moreover, despatch had to be arranged and material for exhibitions provided.

The chemist, with the help of his son-in-law, looked after the chemical diagnostic work and also after the commercial side of the laboratory. I was offered to take over the Professor's job, and accepted. It was well paid and sounded unusual and challenging.

At first I worked part-time, being introduced into the peculiarities of that laboratory's special work by Professor Pribram, but some months later, when my demonstratorship at the university expired in April 1927, I did not apply to have it prolonged, but took up the new work full-time. The Professor soon afterwards left for the United States, and I was in charge.

Magda and I shortly before we got married.

Magda and I with Magda's father shortly before we got married.

Magda and I never became officially engaged, but the news that we were going to be married gradually filtered through. The school she attended had originally been a grammar school for boys only, but over the years a few girls were accepted and in her form there were two. The other girl, whom I never met, was said to be plain and uninteresting, so Magda was the declared favourite. In winter, a week's ski outing was arranged for her form by a young school master, who happened to have been a probationer-teacher at my school many years earlier when I was there. Knowing me and of our engagement, he decided it would be a good thing to have a young doctor on the ski course, and thus invited me to take part. I had never skied before but under the circumstances was ready to try anything, and the boys had a lovely time chaperoning us.

A little later a questionnaire was circularised asking all pupils what they intended to do after school. "To be assistant to my future husband," is what Magda wrote, a thought that made me very happy. The school year drew to an end, and though my earnings were not brilliant, I had proved that I could maintain a wife, and an early marriage was agreed. "We must not consider it the foundation of a new household — it is a bit like grandfather and great aunt moving together into an attic, because it is cheaper than to live apart," was Egon's comment when he signed the consent to the marriage of his daughter,

My wife and I in our first home.

who had not yet come of age, and consequently — according to Austrian law — became not only my wife, but also my ward until she reached the age of 21.

Magda had been brought up as a Lutheran, and the marriage took place in her church three days after she passed her matriculation. A large number of her school friends were present and also the headmaster who, on the last day of term, had announced: "I shall go to church and kiss the girl's hand to demonstrate that she is now grown up." He did! There were no wedding photographs; my bride thought the idea old fashioned!

The little flat in which we settled after our honeymoon was a far cry from an attic. Two rooms, comfortably furnished, a large bathroom and in the beginning we even had a maid-cook. Magda went to cookery classes and the idea was that she would order the food each day which she had learned to cook the day before, thus hiding from the servant her lack of knowledge. It does not seem to have worked. Soon the maid became overbearing, and when one day Magda told her that the mending of a nightdress was untidily done, she replied: "Nobody looks at you in the night anyway." This, to a young bride, appeared to be obvious insolence, and we decided we would be much better on our own. I gave her notice.

It was in the first few weeks that we had the only two rows in our marriage which I can remember — and a little later both made me laugh. The first was when one evening I came home and found that Magda was out and did not come home until much later than I had expected. I was frantic with worry and just about to ring the police to report her missing when, at that moment, she walked in with a radiant smile. I shouted at her. I suppose it was a bit like a mother shouting "Do take care" to a child who stumbles, but really is worried that the child has hurt itself. Magda's explanation was quite simple: she had met some friends from her recent school days who had asked her to go to the cinema with them, and she had forgotten all about being married with a husband waiting anxiously at home. Later on I could not help laughing: after all what can one expect if one marries a schoolgirl!

The second row was when Magda made extravagant use of her newly gained adult freedom and put on lipstick rather thicker than necessary or to my taste. I seized the lipstick and threw it out of the window. The episode ended sadly for me by my going downstairs to recover and bring back the lipstick. But I suppose it saved later battles before they began!

At the onset I found work in Professor Pribram's laboratory very interesting. There was the diagnostic part, which had been almost routine to me previously but which now was taking on a new dimension, not being for long-term research, but for the treatment of acute illness, and thus stirring my clinical interest. There was the handling of and the responsiblity for rare and highly dangerous micro-organisms, and there was a fair amount of work for exhibitions. For those, cultures had to be implanted in a special way into plates which could be mounted on stands where they would be seen to advantage. It appealed to my sense of neatness to do these specimens to perfection, and I was very angry when a mould intruded and spoilt the culture, dissolving some of it. Little did I know that I had, at my fingertips, one of the greatest discoveries ever made in medicine, that this dissolving had a practical implication which was much more important than all the exhibitions. In retrospect, my only comfort that I did not then think of the implications of penicillin is that all the famous bacteriologists familiar with the same phenomenon did not think of the implications either. It took the genius of Sir Alexander Fleming of St Mary's Hospital, London, to recognise the signifi-cance of that action, and later that of Sir Howard Florey, of Oxford, to develop the practical implications of penicillin, the drug which, with its ramifications, is now the greatest saver of life.

However, gradually I found that the work was very repetitive and above all a "dead-end" job. Though I did some scientific work, it was not of the kind to which I was used. I developed a simple apparatus for the breeding of anaerobic bacilli, suitable for small laboratories like ours, which could not afford extensive and expensive implements, but experimental work of clinical significance was impossible. Moreover, though it was by now almost certain that Professor Pribram would stay in the United States and I would become a partner, the laboratory was mainly a business proposition and though affording security, it was not suit-able for a major development. It was possible, as far as one could foresee then, to make a permanent living but it would never offer a real career. I explained that to the family and told them that, if my medical career was to end there, I might just as well do without a medical career altogether. I wondered if Magda's uncle, brother of her mother and father of Bianca who, later, with her husband Oscar Blum-Gentilomo, helped me on my way to England, would take me into his firm. Walter Stross was one of the leading industrialists in textiles, being head of a respected firm founded by his grandfather. There did not seem to be anybody very close to him in the firm and I thought a young, enthusiastic and energetic man might be welcome, particularly as he always seemed to have had a liking for me, as indeed I had for him, mixed with respect and almost admiration. He thought things over, and then decided that, as I had proved myself in medicine, I should continue in that career. However, he also agreed that the job in Professor Pribram's laboratory did not offer a suitable future for my ambitions, energy and what he believed to be my gifts. He suggested a family consortium which should finance my transition to practical medicine and he very generously headed this consortium, which provided me with an income that would keep up our standard of living until I became independent again. Nobody was to hurry me, it was a long-term proposition. Consequently, I gave notice and left the laboratory, and with it theoretical medicine, in June 1928. Thus to Walter Stross and his daughter Bianca, more than to anybody or anything else, I owe whatever I have since achieved and indeed my whole livelihood.

My immediate aim was to gain acceptance for a rotating internship at one of the hospitals which had a particularly good reputation, and my choice was the Krankenhaus Wieden where the head of the surgical department was the very famous Professor Schnitzler, brother of the playwright and novelist, Arthur. Now that I had left theoretical medicine, I reverted to my original idea of becoming a surgeon. At those hospitals there was a waiting list for such internships and one had to serve a preliminary time as volunteer — a kind of guest doctor, called a "hospitant". As such one worked under strict supervision, but the actual work was essentially the same as that of the junior house officers and, depending on the chief's recommendation, selection was made to enter the internship rota as vacancies occurred. I spent this probationary period at the surgical department trying to do and learn as much as possible but, of course, there was still some spare time which I used for research work based on the Institute for Light Biology. Two publications, one in conjunction with a university skin clinic, date from those days.

When, on June 1st 1929, I was appointed a junior houseman, my first six month posting was to the department of gynaecology and obstetrics, which again was headed by an internationally famed Professor (Halban). For me personally more important was the fact that an old friend of mine, who in his student days had been the chairman of the Medical Students' Annual Ball and in whose house the sorry episode of my drunkenness had occurred, was at that time the senior assistant. He very kindly saw to it that I could make the most of my appointment, giving me special opportunities to see and learn more than one usually did in that junior post. We had also published a joint research paper from the department.

A nine month appointment, again to the surgical department, followed, and by that time I had managed to draw the attention of Professor Schnitzler to myself and my interest in surgery which, again, gave me special chances for gaining extra knowledge and experience.

I also kept up research work, and continued to do so during the rest of my time in hospital, mainly about surgical problems, in all having 12 research papers published. One of the papers described unusual findings after a short circuit operation on the intestines. At the time of its publication von Eiselsberg, whom I have mentioned before, was celebrating his 70th birthday and the surgical periodical, which brought out a festival issue on that occasion, decided they would publish the paper in this volume, as it was a matter in which the Professor took a special interest. I was later told that when he read the paper he called his assistants together asking about me and where I worked, as he remembered me only vaguely by name and wondered how I had come to contribute to the festival issue. Having got the information asked for, he wrote me a very nice note of thanks with his photograph, which I still have among my possessions.

In those days we had no professional anaesthetists but one of the house surgeons acted as such, being selected by the surgeon at the beginning of each operating session. I became the chief's favourite anaesthetist for major operations and was actually the first in the department to use intravenous anaesthesia, but our usual method was open-mask ether anaesthetic. One day my privileged position received a sharp shock. During the amputation of a leg, an old man died so suddenly that I did not give the surgeon any warning. "Deaths on the table are bound to happen," Professor Schnitzler commented, "but you should have noticed the danger signals." I had not noticed any and said so, but obviously I had fallen into disgrace. I spent three unhappy days until the forensic post-mortem was done, and it was found that the death had nothing to do with the anaesthesia but was an embolism, which cannot be foreseen.

I experienced one other such death but not during an operation. The patient was a young pregnant woman with acute appendicitis, a member of a family with whom the Professor was friendly and he therefore had operated himself. She was kept in a side ward with four beds, which was the utmost privacy we could offer in those days. However, one day the other three patients left at the same time. "Isn't it lovely?" the young woman said, "it is soon visiting time, my husband will come to see me, and I must make myself pretty for him." She sat up, combing her hair, fell back, and was dead. People think doctors get hardened to death, but one never gets hardened to the end of a young and promising life.

Anyway, after the post-mortem on the old man had cleared me of all responsibility I was taken back into favour and spent a happy few months at the surgical department. By that time my interest in ultimately gaining an assistantship was recognised and acknowledged by the chief. No promise, of course, at that point, but there was an understanding that my development would be benevolently watched. Professor Schnitzler was known and reputed to be the "physician amongst the surgeons" in Vienna and his idea was that I could learn operating later on, and that I should first have a broad-based general medical education. Accordingly it was arranged that I went through the other departments of the hospital until I later returned to the surgical department as a senior house surgeon. As such I was given a fairly long spell in the casualty department. There was no special casualty officer in those days but one of the senior house surgeons was in charge, calling on one of the assistants when he needed advice, but otherwise using one of the junior house surgeons to assist him in the routine work or, as a matter of fact, in anything he felt competent to undertake himself. Once during every morning the Professor himself came to the casualty department to be shown specially interesting or doubtful cases. The casualty department, being the outpatient department nearest to the entrance of the hospital, was the place to which all patients came if they were not sure to which department they should go, and that gave the chief scope for his particular interest and gift in diagnostics.

There was plenty of interest and variety in the daily casualty work and I remember doing a great number of tendon and even nerve sutures. My particular pride was the case of a school caretaker, who, when cleaning a window, had broken it and cut his wrist to the extent of having one artery, two nerves and several tendons severed. In the end he had full use of his hand, the only after-effect being that whenever he bent the index finger, the thumb closed on it too. However, as these two fingers are used together normally this was only a cosmetic drawback. Other injuries for which I established a particular reputation were foreign bodies which had to be removed under X-ray guidance. There were, of course, many other foreign bodies to be removed from all openings of the body, particularly from the ears and noses of children.

The duty rota for the housemen was supposed to be 8 a.m. to 1 p.m. on two days a week, and on the third day from 8 a.m. until 1 p.m. the next day, while the assistants did the twenty-nine hour duty every other day. Of course, they were disturbed much less frequently as the senior house surgeon was the first on call, and only sent for them when he felt that a case was beyond his competence. They had permanent rooms of their own while the housemen had a duty room. When I was on night duty my wife usually came to have supper with me, and then went home. Home at that time was a small flat nearby. When I left the laboratory we had already given up the flat on the outskirts and moved at first to two unfurnished rooms in a large flat belonging to an old lady who herself occupied two rooms and let four, two to us and two to a young solicitor and his wife. They were a pleasant couple and the old lady was largely invisible, but even so, we were glad when we found a self-contained flat in which we had a kitchen and bathroom to ourselves, and which was within easy walking distance of the hospital.

The afternoons off duty were a theoretical rather than a practical proposition, for work was such that much of the writing-up of patients' histories had to be done in our time off, and apart from that, as mentioned before, I continued with my research work. However, on those afternoons off I usually got home in the evening at a fairly reasonable time, which gave some opportunity for home and social life. Thus the doctors were still much better off than the nurses. Most of the State hospitals in Vienna, ours included, were staffed by nuns who lived in a wing of the hospital which served as their convent. They seem to have been on duty, or at least on call, at all hours. I well remember our ward sister once having mentioned she would not be on duty that afternoon, but when I went to the ward to do some paper work she was there. When I queried her presence on her half-day off she said: "If it is my afternoon off I have to go to the sewing room; I prefer to continue nursing." I suppose the responsibility of being in charge of the ward gave her the opportunity of choice. I found nuns as nurses a great boon. There was never any clock-watching, never any desire to be off-duty, and, except for times of communal prayer in the chapel attached to the hospital, when only a skeleton staff remained on duty, we were never short of nurses. If we were busy in the night — and we were busy because no hospital rota existed for admissions, and everybody was taken in who seemed to need hospital attention — even if it meant putting up emergency beds — the duty sister sent round to the convent to ask for as many more nurses as she needed and they would be awoken and would appear in the ward in next to no time. I got on extremely well with these nurses, and although at that time I was not a Christian, I am sure they not only nursed me, but also prayed me to recovery when I fell seriously ill.

I had infected myself in some septic operation, and developed an abscess on my face. At first I did not lay up with it but continued on duty, protecting the patients by wearing a large linen mask which left only my eyes uncovered. Then rigor set in, a full septicaemia developed, and I had to be admitted. It was before penicillin was thought of, and even sulphanilamide had only just been discovered and the first preparation of this group, prontosil, was still very much in the experimental stage, and caused many side effects due to impurities. My senior surgeon very fortunately decided not to use this drug but to give me the usual treatment we had for septicaemia which was alcohol. We used to give it in intravenous injections, I cannot now remember the strength or the quantity, but the results overall were good; I well remember a case of a young woman with puerperal fever to whom one night I gave an injection. Under the influence of the alcohol she quickly became not only cheerful but also gained strength in an amazing way. She jumped out of bed, ran down the stairs and we had to ring the doorman of the hospital quickly to close the outer doors. It was then hide and seek in the dark around the yards of the hospital until we found her and coaxed her back to bed. She recovered.

My own case, however, was that of a staphylococcal septicaemia which had the highest mortality of them all. Overall, it was at that time 75% and if no secondary abscesses developed like empyema it was supposed to be well over 90%. I did not develop an empyema, the only secondary abscess being a fairly superficial one on the surface of a rib. I also pleaded with my senior surgeon not to give me alcohol by injection because this occasionally caused numbness in the fingers and I was still hoping to become a surgeon. He consented. "We still have four bottles of champagne left in the dispensary from the time an attempt was made on the life of our Chancellor. This is the moment to prescribe it," he said, and he duly did it for me. My colleagues who came to visit me had a good deal of the champagne, but then evidently had a bad conscience, and I was brought any amount of wine, champagne and cognac from them and from other well-wishers, so that when I eventually recovered and returned home, I took a taxi-load of drink with me with which we entertained our guests for many months.

At the height of my illness I felt so weak that I had difficulty in holding a pencil to mark the menu, which was sent up from the kitchen every day. I did not eat very much and very little of what I did eat remained with me; I felt or was sick most of the time, but kept cheerful. This my colleagues later on explained by saying that they thought I had not been sober for any time during the six weeks! I remember all the heads of the various departments of the hospital coming together to visit me, among them Professor Sternberg (famed for the description of the characteristic cells in Hodgkin's disease). He was the head of the pathology department of our hospital and said encouragingly, "Hope to see you soon in my department" — correcting himself quickly with "I mean on the first floor" — the ground floor was occupied by the dissecting block! anyway, I was later told that the consultants disagreed only on one point: some thought I would die tomorrow and others the same day. Still, treatment went on including gold injections and blood transfusions, and I confounded all the specialists by eventually recovering. Altogether I was in hospital for eight weeks and needed about four weeks convalescence, but having escaped any major secondary abscess, I had no after-effects whatsoever from my illness.

After my return to duty another round of appointments followed as senior house physician to the medical departments, but by this time it was common knowledge that I was designated to become Assistant to Professor Schnitzler and the various departmental heads and the assistants very kindly gave me the opportunity to make the best possible use of the comparatively short time I spent in their departments. Eventually I returned to the surgical department to be specially trained for the job I was to take on. By then, although the general surgeon was still doing the bulk of urological operations, a special urological outpatient department had been opened at the hospital, and I was seconded to this for a short while. Here I got the opportunity of doing special urological examinations, including not only cystoscopy but also the much more complicated probing of ureters which, in those days, had become firmly the domain of a urological surgeon. I also spent a time in the laryngo-otological outpatient department to become competent in investigations and diagnostics concerning this field. Orthopaedics, of course, belonged in those days to general surgery with only one specialist institution in this field, the Orthopaedic University Clinic under Professor Lorenz, who developed the first operation for congenital hip dislocation. It was only much later that, largely in consequence of Boehler's activities, orthopaedics became established as a specialty on its own. In my time

64

On holiday in Switzerland in 1933.

at the Krankenhaus Wieden we dealt not only with all fractures, but also with a large number of varying orthopaedic cases.

During that time, an old gypsy woman attended the hospital and persuaded me to have my hand read. "You won't stay long at this hospital," she said, "and later on will be very glad of it." What nonsense I thought. My mind was on the Assistantship, which by now had been promised to me by the Chief, and that meant years more at the hospital. It later transpired that the gypsy woman was quite right. Altogether I am rather inclined to believe in the gift of some gypsies to read the future. As a very young man, in the People's Prater, I had been told by another gypsy that I would have three children and that I should always find people who enjoyed working for me. I certainly have the three children, and from the fact that nobody in my employ, whom I myself liked, left me except under pressure of external circumstances, and my last secretary had been with me for almost twenty-three years until her death in April 1981, I assume that the second part also was true.

As I said initially there was a usual period of four years for any rotating internship. However, if anybody was designated to take on a post of assistant and the vacancy only occurred in the following year, provision was made to have this period extended to a fifth year. This was so in my case, and hence I got

65

My wife with my mother in our first garden.

prolongation from June 1st 1933 to May 31st 1934, the Assistantship actually falling vacant on July 1st, when, pending the definite appointment which had to come officially from the Ministry of Health, I was provisionally appointed Acting Assistant.

I got on very well with all my colleagues, but in particular with Dr Hogenauer, the other assistant, who had now become the senior and acted for the Chief in his absence. This was not very often as Professor Schnitzler, when he was at home, wanted to be informed by telephone, even at night, of any major incident to decide whether he would come himself to operate or anyway give advice as to what should be done.

Normally the work was shared equally between the assistants, one looking after the male patients, the other after the female wards, changing over every three months. However, as Hogenauer had been assistant for many years and knew I was keen on widening my experience in operating, he said I could do any operations I liked, from his wards as well, excluding of course those that Professor Schnitzler did himself. He also offered to assist me in any operation which I did not yet feel competent to tackle with only juniors assisting me. Thus I was very busy and very happy.

Then the thunderbolt struck!

Assistants on the Viennese public hospitals were appointed on the nominations of the heads of all departments, and they automatically accepted the wish of the prospective chief. All major public hospitals in Vienna being State-controlled, the appointment had to be signed and thus confirmed by the Ministry of Health. That had never been other than a formality. Not so this time.

66

The Minister of Health at that time, though in the Cabinet of Chancellor Dollfuss, was a Nazi sympathiser. How he got into it I would not know, but I do know that not very long after the, for me, critical date, he was dropped from it as his ideas were incompatible with those of the remainder of the Cabinet. Anyway, he was in charge at the time. He refused to countersign my appointment, and appointed a friend of his, a Nazi, transferring him from another hospital to ours, a procedure never before heard or thought of. I was informed on July 26th that, as from August 1st this other man would be coming to fill the post of Assistant and my appointment as Acting Assistant would come to an end at that date. Not only that, but as my fifth year as hospital doctor had been granted on condition that the vacancy for Assistant would arise, which I was to fill, my time of service was to end on the same day. The bottom had fallen out of my world; all my plans had come to nothing, and I still marvel today how I avoided despair. Still, youth is resilient; I always have been an optimist, and I immediately made plans to build a new future. Three things probably helped.

The whole procedure was so unheard of that everybody I knew not only expressed sympathy, but also a readiness to help. I immediately made an application to our Superintendent, quoting a regulation according to which hospital doctors had to be given six months in their final service year to build up their private practice. The Superintendent was very helpful and, over the telephone, at once succeeded in getting a provisional three months prolongation, which later on a written application was extended to the full six months. Thus I had the opportunity to perfect my all-round experience at the various medical departments and, of course, to draw my salary until May 31st 1934. The heads of all departments were extremely friendly and obliging, and gave me every opportunity to do the work I wanted, permitting me at the same time to regulate my duty times according to my requirements.

My own Chief, who was on holiday at the time, wrote to me expressing his disappointment and commiseration but, of course, the law was against us, and there was nothing to do but to accept it. I was later told that he and Dr Trevani, his new assistant, got on very badly, and it was not very long before Professor Schnitzler, who had reached retiring age, but not yet compulsory retiring age, resigned from the hospital. I do not know how his successor and Dr Trevani got on, but ultimately my job certainly brought him no luck. Having been a Nazi, he suddenly changed his colours to become a pronounced Austrian Patriot. I suppose, as a token of his earnestness, he denounced our instrument maker who consequently lost his contract as supplier to the hospital. He was the man whom I mentioned before, who, though secretly a Nazi, had offered me all the help he could, but he never forgave Dr Trevani, as he himself told me. When the Nazis occupied Austria he now, in his turn, denounced Dr Trevani as a traitor to the Party. He was arrested and hanged himself in the police cell.

Chapter 6
MY MEDICAL PRACTICE IN VIENNA

A great help in bearing my disappointment and retaining confidence in the future was the fact that, just then, belief in God had taken on a new meaning for me. I had always believed in a power beyond us to whom we bore responsibility, but organised religion had meant little to me.

Of the Jewish religion I knew very little, but I always felt it to be somehow incomplete with its indefinite waiting for the Messiah. I know much more of it since I became a Christian, and can appreciate why they do not believe in Christ as the Messiah. This is illustrated by the story told of one of the great Rabbis at the time of Christ's birth. When told the Messiah had been born he excitedly got up from his studies, looked out into the street and saw two people quarrelling. "The Messiah has not come," he said sadly, for according to Jewish belief, with the arrival of the Messiah, all difficulties will automatically be smoothed out and everything will be wonderful. According to Christian belief, however, Christ the Messiah just opened the way, but each and everyone of us will have to walk it ourselves to reach eternal happiness which, to me, seems more in accord with creatures of free will.

Christianity, which in Vienna at that time meant mainly Catholicism, had always attracted me. There was the culture which seemed so natural and which would not have made sense without its basis in religion. Then there was the ceremonial of the Church. I had occasionally slipped into High Mass with music, and though I did not really understand what was going on, I was impressed by the joy the service radiated. There was praise, thanksgiving and jubilation, and the words "We give you thanks, we praise you for your glory" impressed me then and are still something ingrained in my belief.

Around this critical time I had, under the influence of my wife's father, joined a small international esoteric Christian sect led by a Swiss who, under the name of Bo Yin Ra, wrote books which were full of common sense and rules for a good life based on belief in God. The belief and practice of this sect was said to be founded on the tradition of John, as distinct from the Petrine tradition which Bo Yin Ra considered erroneous. After all, had it not been John who was the disciple whom our Lord loved? The logic was that it was to him Christ would have told his innermost thoughts. How Bo Yin Ra was supposed to know of them and to hand on the teaching I never discovered, but not knowing much of the Church I accepted what I was told, eager to learn something of Christianity and happy and confident in the security that, as long as I did my best, God was watching over me and all would come right in the end.

I think there was also the prophesy of the gypsy which contributed to my confidence. "You will leave the hospital soon, and later on will be very glad

My wife with our firstborn daughter.

about it." I was determined to make that come true, to build a future for my family and myself, to turn my unique misfortune into a unique opportunity, and to build up a life and a practice different from any other doctor. Speaking of family, as if as a token of my regained vitality and trust in the future, it was just then that my wife conceived our first child Gabriele, who was born on October 26th 1934.

Practically, my first task was to find a flat which was suitable for the practice I pictured, and I found one which appeared to be ideal. Situated in one of the two best districts of Vienna, it consisted of five huge rooms, four of them with three windows each, a kitchen, bathroom and two servants' rooms, one of which served as a spare room. There was a big entrance hall separating the main flat from the servants' quarters. It was all very elegant, very attractive, very expensive and my family was evidently very worried when I decided that this was where I could see myself succeeding. But, in spite of the worries, they stood by me and helped. The smallest main room I furnished as an examination/operating room, the next room was a sitting-cum-consulting room, the next a dining-cum-waiting room, and then there came an oddly shaped many-angled corner room which we used as a bedroom; from there, lying in bed, we could see the green cupola of the famous St Charles Church. The fifth room was soon to be put into use as a nursery, and we had a maid who stayed with us from the first day to the last of our stay in the flat and proved a real treasure. The furniture came from the various members of the family, much from my own mother who then lived in a very small flat and had had to part with many of the large, mostly antique, pieces for which we had ample space. The examination room, with its sober, very practical and clinical equipment, was in startling contrast to the comfort of the other rooms to which the patients were admitted. The practice I expected was a fashionable one, something one would find in the best parts of Kensington or Chelsea, and as there would never be very many in the waiting room at any one time, there was no reason not to let them use the furniture we ourselves used. Such arrangements were very usual at that time among family doctors in Vienna.

The story of how I had been forced into general practice, the connections of our families and a knowledge of my long and very thorough training had all become common knowledge and helped to start the practice. Moreover, I was well within walking distance of my old hospital and many of my former hospital patients who could afford it now came to me, privately, encouraged by the nursing nuns. However, the biggest contribution to my future career came from my old Chief, Professor Schnitzler, who spoke about me to one of his former assistants, the surgeon Dr Emil Schwarzmann. Schwarzmann was one of the few Jewish surgeons who were well known in the whole city and had a very busy practice, being largely called for consultation and operations by Jewish doctors who were all appalled and enraged at the injustice done to me. They were very willing to help, and Schwarzmann offered to take me on as his private assistant when I left hospital. This meant he was taking me with him to assist at most of his private operations for a fee that usually amounted to 5% of his own operation fee. The so-called first assistance was usually performed by the referring general practitioner, it carried a fee of 10% of the operation fee, and as it was forbidden in Austria, as here, to pay a referral commission, it seemed to be a good legal way out of the dilemma to invite those doctors to assist at the operation.

The trouble was that some of them had really no idea of surgery and it was very often up to me, as the second assistant, to act as first assistant as well. This was not always easy because, traditionally, the first assistant stands at the table opposite the operator where he has much more mobility than the second assistant, who stands on the surgeon's left. As Schwarzmann could not very well grumble at the family doctor for fear of upsetting him and not getting any more referrals, he grumbled at me, hoping that some of those things which he asked of me and which I could not very easily do, the family doctor might wake up to. Still all the grumbling and occasional bickering did not harm our basic friendship which quickly developed, and I remember that on Schwarzmann's 50th birthday on August 2nd 1935, I gave him a little good-luck plaque for his car showing a little dog. It was accompanied by a poem I made up bemoaning the life of a dog who is kicked for things that are not his fault but who still remains faithful. The boss seemed to appreciate my gift and it became a standing joke between us.

I took over as assistant to Schwarzmann the day I left hospital and he at once got me appointed as assistant to the First Public Children's Sick Institute, a charitable institution. It was an honorary appointment but it gave me official status. When later on in Spring 1935, he was also appointed honorary head of the surgical department of the Mariahilfer Hospital and Clinic, he also had me appointed as honorary assistant there.

In the Children's Institute all the children were operated on as outpatients, which meant that we could not do the really major operations. However, we performed not only circumcisions but also operations for hernia, kryptorchism (undescended testicles) and even some appendicectomies. Of course we needed a theatre sister and were fortunate in finding a lady who had been trained as a nurse during the first world war, had fallen in love with nursing and was ready to do everything, not only voluntarily but very often paying for things out of her own pocket. She was the wife of a well-to-do Austrian solicitor, and we three couples — Schwarzmanns, Glaessners and we — soon became firm friends and saw a lot of each other, even outside the hospital. After the occupation of Austria the Glaessners emigrated to the U.S.A., he, after a time managing to establish some kind of law practice, but when Mr Glaessner eventually died, I gradually lost contact with her, and it seems Schwarzmann did too. He mentioned her less and less in his letters, and since he died I have not heard any more either about Mrs Glaessner or any of the Schwarzmann family.

Small children were, after the operation, taken home in the pram, older ones in taxis, lying across the parents' laps, and quite often I went with them.

In doing not only minor operations on outpatients, we followed a Scottish publication and we thought it was the normal practice in Britain. Great was my surprise when, after coming to this country, I found that my relevant ideas were considered a Viennese peculiarity. Evidently the example of the Scottish surgeon had not invited a large following and certainly not in England. I always visited patients who needed it at their home and the parents always had my private telephone number to call me at any time of the day or night. Of course it meant for me some effort and expense, but overall not only my earnings through the private assistantship, but also the laying of the foundation of my future practice in which surgery played a major role, made it all very worth while.

The Mariahilfer Hospital was a small private hospital, but it gave opportunities to operate on and treat in-patients, though most of the major private operations my Chief did in one of the two leading private nursing homes in the city.

My general practice grew steadily. Several elderly ladies — some of them friends of grandparents or aunts — turned to me as their doctor as somehow or other I was talked about in the city, and I quickly got the reputation of a go-ahead doctor who even tackled his own surgical and orthopaedic cases. I particularly remember one lady who had fallen and broken her arm, who until then still had kept to the doctor of her youth, though he was mainly interested in children and young people. It was slightly embarrassing as, at that time, he was the medical superintendent of the Children's Sick Institute where I worked, but gracefully and seemingly very pleased to rid himself of a case which was evidently outside his scope, he handed her over to me and did not mind that she continued to remain my patient. I got lovely and generous Christmas presents from her and, when eventually she died in old age, she had left me some money, all the pictures on one wall of her drawing room, and a Venetian chandelier. She had been to my consulting rooms once, just to see them, otherwise I visited her at her home, but on this occasion she had remarked that the chandelier in the dining/waiting room was too small for the large room, and the ornate furniture, and she mentioned in her will that the Venetian chandelier was meant to replace it.

Another patient whom I shall always remember was a step-daughter of the Waltz King, Johann Strauss. She was an asthmatic who often needed an injection at night, and particularly wanted one whenever she had been to the opera, which was very often. For me that meant being ready for a late evening call when she got home, but she was not only delighted to pay the fee but also recommended me to many of her friends, so one way and another my general practice steadily grew.

Even so, I usually had time to accompany Schwarzmann to the large surgical outpatient department of the Workman's Sick Insurance, of which he was in charge, to assist him with treatment, and as that was almost every week-day, I was soon a familiar figure to patients, nurses and administrative staff. Thus no objections were raised when I occasionally acted on the Chief's behalf if, at the last minute, he was prevented from attending. In time, this became an accepted procedure and I was allowed to act in his stead even during his holidays, although I was not officially classed as a specialist. In consequence, it was also accepted that I acted for another of Schnitzler's former assistants (Withold von Schey), who was surgical consultant to the Sickness Insurance of the Merchant Guild.

As the birth of our first child was approaching I had a discussion with my wife who had been brought up a Lutheran, but actually had hardly ever practised her religion. I did not know much about the Lutheran beliefs except that they had grown out of a protest against the Catholic Church, which I had come more and more to love and admire. I had no doubt that some of Luther's complaints about abuses in the Church were justified, but I always thought they had been the wrongs of individuals and that the Church as such could not be blamed for them. Moreover, I always had an instinctive aversion to protest movements which lead to a break with the original institution. I was quite aware that reforms are necessary at times but always admired those who succeeded in reforming the church from inside, like St Francis of Assisi, rather than by founding separatist movements. In those days of persecution of the Jews I myself would not have even considered leaving the Jewish community, though I did not feel any affinity with it. According to Austrian law, however, children had to be brought up in the religion of one of the parents, and I suggested to my wife the choice of becoming a Catholic or having the child brought up in the Jewish religion. It was an easy decision for my wife because she herself had never felt quite at home with the Lutheran religion; she was profoundly impressed by the Christian culture, which in Austria was, of course, almost entirely Catholic, and most of our friends were Catholics. She was instructed by one of our Benedictine friends who was a professor for history at the Vienna University, but the teaching was not very thorough because he only really drew her attention to the differences between the Protestant and the Catholic faiths, assuming that she knew all about the Protestant faith which she did not. Thus she became a Catholic a few months before our daughter was born, but in the first instance it did not make any great difference to our lives.

It was not much later that the leader of our Viennese esoteric group told me he was sending me an interesting patient, a Professor von Hildebrand, the leading Catholic philosopher in the city. None of us could foresee how meeting him was to change my future life. I treated him for some minor complaint, but we also got talking, and he invited me to a circle he had established with friends in his house, where every fortnight philosophical problems were discussed. I was fascinated and in my spare time read a lot of philosophical books with theological implications.

Consequently, Hildebrand also invited me to another circle held on the alternate fortnightly evenings to which only his more intimate friends had access. The result of my reading was that I started to recognise that the things I assented to in our Johanneic group were those identical with the Petrine tradition, but where they differed I believed more and more in the Church's teaching. However, I still thought that assent to the teaching of the Church was all that was required and that baptism was a mere formality. Then I read a magazine edited by the Rev. John Oesterreicher, a convert Jew himself, who originally had been a medical student. I felt I wanted to talk to him and asked Hildebrand where I could find him. "Nothing easier," he said. "He is the senior curate at the church next door but one to where you live. I know him well, send him a note and introduce yourself as one of my friends."

I did just that. Father Oesterreicher was a very busy man, he was a well known preacher, and also ran a mission for Jews called Opus St Pauli besides his normal parish work. All the same he was willing to spare me some time for talks but said they would have to be in my house as his parish priest did not want visitors at the Presbytery in the evening, the only time he could manage. I was delighted, nothing could have suited me better, and a long and beautiful friendship developed out of these talks. In time, Father Oesterreicher got into the habit of inviting his friends into our house rather than to the Presbytery, and in consequence we met a number of very interesting priests, like Father Dillersberger who wrote a very well known commentary on St Mark's Gospel, the dominican Father Franciscus Stratmann who wrote on the Church and Peace, and Dom Sugnol, a leading expert in Gregorian chant. They came for meals and long talks.

At first Father Oesterreicher and I, Magda being present, had general theological and philosophical discussions, but it gradually dawned on me that baptism was of the essence, and I underwent real instruction. During these instructions, which were very thorough, I realised more and more that the faith of the Church is one and indivisible and baptism indispensable to it. I suppose it helped that I clearly realised that in the eyes of the Nazis I would remain Jew even if baptised,

73

My wife in 1936.   Father (now Mgr.) John Oesterreicher in 1937.

and that, therefore, my decision to be received into the Church was in no way an attempt to escape trouble. It was summer by the time my instruction ended and Father Oesterreicher said to me: "Now think of a feast on which you would like to be baptised in autumn when I come back from my holidays. If you should die before then you will be considered a Catholic through baptism of desire. Meanwhile I have a young Protestant under instruction to whom I have to give the last three talks, will you do that for me, instruct him and I shall examine him when I come back before he is received into the Church. But don't tell him you have not yet been baptised yourself." This reminded me of the days when on a very different level Professor Stoerk said, appointing me as demonstrator, "But don't tell the students that you have not yet sat your own examinations."

By that time I had, of course, resigned from our esoteric group.

St Michael's feast on September 29th 1936, was the great day. Magda, who had been attending the instruction and now at last really knowing something about the Catholic faith, had become as convinced and eager as myself, made for me a full length "white garment" which I have kept ever since, and in which I hope to be buried. I was received with the full ceremonial baptism for adults in Latin at the convent of our Lady of Sion. At baptism I added Michael to my Christian names and, ever since, have insisted that this third name be quoted whenever possible. Hildebrand was my Godfather, and he and his friends came to sing the Mass of thanksgiving when I received my first Holy Communion.

74

That evening, Hildebrand and his friends came to a meal at our house, and for the first of many times, we said together Benedictine Compline. Hildebrand was very knowledgeable and keen on liturgy, and had many friends among the Benedictines, and I suppose this awoke an echo in me, though I had already, earlier, developed a particular liking for the Mass at the "Schotten Stift", a Benedictine house and school in Vienna. Hildebrand himself, however, was a Franciscan Tertiary, as was his brother-in-law, the well known sculptor, Theodor Georgii (known to his friends as Fedja) with whom I also made friends. They both had a leaning towards poverty and the simple life, whilst I cannot say that I had any hankering for it. As I later proved, I could put up with primitive living and poverty if I had to, but it was never something I would choose. The Benedictines were, and still remain, my ideal. I am now an Oblate of Buckfast Abbey.

What I had not anticipated was that the Jewish doctors would take a very hostile view of my being baptised, though I later understood their attitude. After all, I had been the outstanding example of injustice to the Jews, they had all rallied round me and tried to help, and now they considered me a deserter if not a traitor. Schwarzmann told me that many of the family doctors with whom he worked refused to work with me any longer, and therefore, he could not take me as his assistant to private operations in which they participated. It meant a noticeable financial loss, but in a way I was glad to feel that I had made a sacrifice for my new faith. Moreover, as always, when one door closes another opens. My practice grew steadily, two old doctors in the neighbourhood asked me to help them out, and my Chief himself did not alter his attitude to me at all. Though himself a Jew from Smyrna (probably originally from Spain) he upheld me where he could, was evidently fond of me, and appreciated my motives. He even went to the length of sending me patients to operate upon for appendicitis, hernia and other similar cases, telling patients who came to him for an operation, but appeared to be rather taken aback by his considerable fees, "Have it done by my assistant, he will do it as well but much cheaper."

It was a happy time without worries, both the general and surgical practice steadily increasing. We had a lot of social life in those days, the practice bringing more social contacts and the social contacts bringing more patients. Our maid Resi was perfect in every respect. When we had guests — which was often — the meal was prepared and served perfectly. She was very good with our small daughter who liked her, but still put on a little act whenever we went out in the evening. "I feel a pressure that makes me want to cry" ("es drueckt mich zum weinen") she used to complain, but nothing much came of it so the heartless parents did not take particular notice. Then one day I watched Gabriele playing mother and child with her doll. "I go out with Daddy tonight," Mummy Gabriele said. "Es drueckt mich zum weinen," was the doll's reply. "Then blow your nose," Mummy Gabriele said sternly. The next time Gabriele said to us "es drueckt mich zum weinen" I said, taking a leaf out of her book, "then blow your nose!" A big beaming smile from Gabriele — who appreciated the situation

— and nothing further was heard about any temptation to cry when ever we went out in the evenings. Children!

Resi was also perfect for the practice. She kept the place spotlessly clean, including the instruments, and as besides my general practice in those days I did a lot of minor surgery at home, and quite a bit of gynaecological treatments, there was a lot of cleaning up to do. She also had an excellent memory which helped me because, even when I was young, I often did not remember my patients' names. In those days I received a lot of paintings from my patients, most of them of no special value, though treasured possessions of the donor, and I certainly did not feel like hanging them permanently. Resi not only told me who was in the waiting room, but also remembered if there was one who had given me a picture, and without comment brought in the picture to hang on a pre-destined hook, where it remained until the consultation was over. It was then taken back into the spare room among the others.

Politically, of course, we were to some extent affected by the Nazi regime being in power in Germany, but the longer time went on, and particularly since the murder of Chancellor Dollfuss left Austria intact, most people discounted the possibility of Austria falling victim. The Nazi movement did not appear to be very strong, and, as a matter of fact, I am still convinced that it was not very strong and had it not been for the military might and recklessnes of the German neighbours it would never have become so. But then it suddenly happened. Without the threat and pressure of the Nazis imported from Germany, Austria, which had a very strong tradition of its own culture, would not have succumbed, but in the event Austria did fall. It was a forceful occupation which the Germans made to appear as a voluntary joining ("Anchluss"). I think my experience during those days, which I described at the start of this book, prove how many Austrians acted only unwillingly under severe pressure.

Hildebrand had always emphasised that one of the main Christian virtues is to be ready for any change ("Veraenderungsbereitschaft"). In this I certainly proved to be his pupil. A few days before, I had been a prosperous doctor with a lovely home, a happy family, and a promising future. Now I found myself a homeless refugee with a quite uncertain future, just one trunk full of clothing for a family of three, and the sum of £3.10s., which was all we were allowed to take with us. Still, I was young, energetic — and despair was never something I was inclined towards. Though I was doubtful that I would ever be able to continue in medicine, I was confident that I could build up a future for us somehow, and the very likely prospect that Magda and I would have to act as a caretaker couple or valet/housekeeper to a rich person in England (I always hoped to go to England) did not frighten or dishearten me. For the next few weeks, up to three months, I felt we were safe anyway, as our cousins had guaranteed us for that period which was the longest permitted by Swiss law, and had invited us to use their house as our temporary home. The £3.10s. just got us there!

Chapter 7
INTERLUDE IN SWITZERLAND

Bianca, as I have mentioned before, is my wife's first cousin, the daughter of Walter Stross, who had helped me in the days of transition from laboratory work to practical medicine, and whom I have to thank for being able to continue my work as a doctor. Oscar was Viennese by birth, with an Italian mother. I had known him in Vienna before either of us was married, but had not seen him for many years, as he was living in Switzerland where he was partner in a private bank. Oscar and Bianca had a lovely newly built house, which was beautiful but in no way showy, and fitted the landscape perfectly. When we arrived, we were treated as very welcome visitors, and apart from the fact that Oscar gave me some pocket money so that I should not run about with completely empty pockets, there was nothing in their attitude and hospitality to remind us of our state as homeless refugees. However, whenever I myself brought up the subject of our situation and asked for advice as to what I might do to further my chances, I found every assistance and understanding. Letter writing continued with the help of Bianca, who then spoke English better than I, and gradually the chances appeared to improve for me to be admitted to England for requalification.

Then a letter came from Hester Colles, telling me that she and her husband, with a friend, were going to visit the upper Italian lakes; could I come and meet them there as it was so much easier to recommend a person one knew personally. I replied that unfortunately it was impossible for me to do this because my visa for Switzerland only allowed for transit, even if with a three month stay; once I had left Switzerland by any frontier I could not return. Never mind, was the reply, then we shall come and see you.

That was how Hester and Harry Colles and their friend, Anna Coltman, entered my life. Harry was exactly how I had always pictured an English gentleman. Tall, broad-shouldered, with a slight stoop and greying hair — he was about 59 years old — clad in a grey flannel suit. Hester was small, her hair too was greying, but her lively movements and speech made her appear much younger than her age. She must have been then about 46, that is about ten years older than I. Anna was much taller, white haired, looking austere and angular. I never knew her age, but she gave the impression of being an old lady.

Hester was full of ideas and plans, but always referred to Harry to ask his opinion which invariably confirmed hers. He was a man of few words, but one had the impression that her referring to him as the ultimate authority was very genuine, and that they had actually made plans together beforehand. It always remained like that. Whatever we discussed she said: "I shall ask Harry," and then the verdict came: "Harry says . . . ." However, Hester was always the immediate helper and later on, when she gave our elder daughter the book "Johny Crow",

Oscar and Bianca Blum Gentilomo who sheltered us on our journey to England.

it struck me that this was the perfect description of herself. She always was Johny Crow, ready with any assistance needed.

That afternoon in Lugano three major decisions were taken. Harry and Hester took with them a Curriculum Vitae which I had prepared in German to have it translated, several copies made and then send it to anybody who might be willing and able to help in getting me selected for study and requalification. Meanwhile I was to write to the Secretary of the Scottish Medical Board, telling him that I had applied for permission to study and would like to obtain my British degree in Scotland. The third was that Hester and Harry would enquire what books I needed for my first examinations (Pathology and Pharmacology) and would send me the books so that I could spend the waiting time in Switzerland usefully studying for those examinations, even though one could not yet be certain whether I would be allowed to take them.

Soon the books arrived and I started studying for the pathology examination. The book on "Materia Medica" (pharmacology) was a puzzle to me as I had never seen or heard of drams and ounces or scruples; consquently the signs for them did not mean anything to me, and there was nobody to explain them. The large loggia running along the front of the house on the first floor was given up to me as a study, and with its quietness, fresh but warm air and the peaceful view, could not have been more ideal.

Harry Colles.   Hester Colles.

Time ran on. The end of my three months permission to stay was in sight, and so was the likelihood of my selection for a study visa. The British Government did not like it if one entered the country on a visitor's visa, and then tried to stay for studies, so Hester and Harry warned. "Try and get your stay in Switzerland prolonged until the study visa comes through," they recommended. Oscar managed to get the necessary extension of my stay until I was notified that a study visa had been granted. For my wife there was then no difficulty to get an even further extension, as it had now become clear that she would be allowed to join me at any time; for the time being the Colles advised that I should come on my own until I could be settled. Oscar took me aside and said: "You will need some money to start with," and he gave me a sum saying: "If ever you can repay I shall be pleased, if you can't, forget about it, and consider it as a gift. But you cannot have more." I am happy to say that I repaid the money, but my debt to his kindness and generosity remains.

And now it was goodbye to the family and to Switzerland. The interlude between the two halves of my life had come to an end, and I started the journey into the unknown. It turned out to be for me a journey not only into the unknown but into the undreamt of world of pre-war Britain and a new life, the beginning of which then struck me — and thinking back still strikes me — as a fairy tale.

Chapter 8
NEW START IN ENGLAND

It was Friday October 14th 1938, when I landed in Dover. The Immigration Officer stamped my passport, and then handed me a telegram. It was from Harry Colles, welcoming me to England and saying that Hester would meet me on arrival of the boat train at Victoria Station.

I had slight misgivings when I saw my luggage disappear into the luggage van without a ticket for it; on the Continent one always had to have a receipt for everything. Still, it was a very minor worry, the warmth of Harry's welcome and the expectation of meeting Hester on my arrival in London gave me a feeling of confidence that all would be well. Little did I imagine just how well it would be, and what surprises were in store for me.

The train drew into Victoria Station, and there was Hester with a welcoming smile. "What sort of journey did you have? Have you anything to declare? I will accompany you to the Customs."

"Anything to declare?" asked the Customs Officer. "No," replied Hester for me, "Any camera?" the Officer continued; "No," replied Hester, The Officer turned pointedly to me and repeated his question. "Any camera?" and I replied "No". Without asking me to open my luggage it was marked for passing. I had noticed Hester turning a little red in the face when the Customs Officer repeated his question to me. Now she went up to him and said: "I think it was very wrong of you Officer to ask my friend again if he had a camera when I had already answered for him. What should visitors to this country think if you don't accept the word of a lady." "How did you know Madam?" the Customs Officer retorted. "Because I asked him," was Hester's reply, "and if I had not asked him I would not have answered for him." Now it was the Officer's turn to look embarrassed. "You are quite right madam," he said, "I apologise." This conversation was my first of many great impressions on arrival in this country. I am afraid in Austria at that time everybody would have hooted with laughter at the thought of a Customs Officer accepting the word of a lady, or of offering an apology, and I fear in the Great Britain of today the reaction might be similar.

Hester took me to a taxi. "Do you remember my friend Anna who came with us to Lugano?" she asked. Of course I did. "She is still in the country, and will remain there a little longer. She wondered if, meanwhile, you would like to make use of her town flat, it is just around the corner from us. There is a house-keeper, but she is getting old, so she will only be able to prepare breakfast and one main meal for you. The others you will have to find for yourself."

The taxi stopped in Swan Court, a block of luxury flats. Anna's had a bed-room, a sitting room, the housekeeper's room, kitchen and bathroom. Room had been made for my clothes in one of the wardrobes and in some of the drawers.

"Now unpack and then come for dinner to us," said Hester. "Don't dress tonight, we always dress for dinner, but we won't expect you to do so tonight, as you will have been busy unpacking." She sketched the way for me to reach their flat in Cheyne Walk.

I unpacked as in a dream. Sufficient space had been cleared for my things, but Anna Coltman's belongings were also still around, everything for me to use if I wanted to do so.

When I arrived at the Colles', she was in evening dress, he in dinner jacket, and sherry was offered. Enquiries were made with regard to the end of my time in Lugano, the family and my journey. "You will want to write to Magda of course," said Hester, handing me a small attaché case. "You will find writing paper, postcards, and stamps in there — also some of our money which you will have to get used to." She explained shillings, pounds and pence to me, and there was in the case everything from a farthing to a five pound note, and everything in duplicate so that I could refresh my memory from the spare coin or note in case I had spent some! She also handed me her latch key. "I don't know what sort of books my friend Anna has got, probably nothing much that will interest you. Harry has a large library, let yourself into our flat any time. If we are not at home we shall always be pleased to find you here when we return."

For lunch next day I was invited to Hester's Club (The Forum), and I cannot remember a single time while at Swan Court when I had to find any meal myself. I was always invited out for at least one meal a day. Twice a week I dined with Harry in the Athenaeum Club, (the importance of that Club only gradually dawning on me) and then went with him to a concert in the Queen's Hall. Being the chief musical critic of "The Times" he had always two tickets for every concert. Some evenings I had a very good, if simple, meal in the house of a primary school teacher, on others a formal dinner in one of the big houses. I particularly remember one dinner in the house of Sir Leopold and Lady Savile, who I was assured had been anxious to meet me.

In Swan Court itself I led the life of a rich man, even though I had not a penny to my name. A cooked breakfast every day (I refused early morning tea, not being used to it), "The Times" and "The Daily Telegraph" on the breakfast table, and every meal I had "at home" was excellent in quality and ample enough to make another main meal unnecessary. The dear old housekeeper was attention herself. Meanwhile, I had also come into the possession of some money. From whence it all came I never knew, cheques in those days had no names printed on them and the signatures I could not read. Each time Hester said: "A friend of mine felt she wanted to do something to help you. She wants to remain anonymous and doesn't want any thanks, except through me." Harry took me to Barclays Bank in Chelsea, introduced me to the Manager and so started my first bank account in this country. I have been with Barclays ever since, and received much help from them.

Every day, until my first interview with the Refugee Committee, Hester gave me instructions for the next day. "You must get to know London," and she told

Harry and Ethel Fletcher.

me which bus to take, from which corner, where to get off, where to walk and what to see. Hester thought it was the most sensible way to spend my time pending clarification of my future.

At the Refugee Committee I was informed that the Scottish Medical School was full and now all doctors had to take their re-qualification in England. This meant fewer examinations but two years in hospital instead of one, which was all the Scottish Board required, asking instead for two extra examinations. When Hester heard this she said that I should go myself to Edinburgh and speak to the secretary there. "But the Committee said . . ." I murmured rather weakly, having already come to the conclusion that Hester and Harry were always right. "Never mind what they said, you go and see the secretary" was their firm order. "I shall get your ticket," and the ticket I got for a sleeper with instructions to have breakfast at the Waverley Hotel, where non-residents could also have a bath, and then to go and see the secretary. I was to return the following night by sleeper. I strictly followed my orders. The secretary regretted. The allocation for foreign doctors had been exhausted. Suddenly I had an inspiration. "But I wrote to you from Switzerland asking you to reserve a place for me." "Oh, you are you," he beamed, "We counted you in, you are alright." I was happy, Hester was satisfied, and I informed the Committee that I had booked Scotland already in advance and therefore was on their list. I had no further reply from them.

It was at about this time that Harry and Hester thought that, in spite of Munich, the political situation did not seem very safe and they decided this was not the time for frontiers between married couples. "We have a friend in the country who would like Magda as companion, and does not mind the little girl in the house," they said. "We shall let Magda and Gabriele come over to England on condition that she will go and stay with Mrs Benthall. If you live together you will never pass your examinations and will never learn English." We could not do anything but agree. I met my wife and little daughter for a few hours on their arrival, and off they went to Teignmouth.

My first examinations were to be in December, and for hours every day I pored over my books, taking also a course in Materia Medica which opened my eyes regarding British weights and measures. Pharmacology had never been my strongest subject. But however many hours I spent over the books, I always had my one main meal out.

Time passed and Hester said that Anna would soon return to Town. "Come to tea tomorrow," she added. I said that I really could not spare the time as I had to work, but Hester never took no for an answer. "It is much more important for you to meet people," she insisted. "Friends of mine are coming to tea who want to meet you," and that's how I met the Fletchers. Henry Martineau Fletcher was a famous British architect, one time secretary to the Royal Institute of British Architects. His wife, whom he had married years before as a widower, and who had brought up his two daughters, was an American. After tea she asked if she could have a word with me. "I understand Anna Coltman is soon coming back to town, and you have not yet made up your mind where you will live then," she said, "I have to go to America for some time to visit relations of mine and poor Harry will feel so lonely in the big house on his own. Could you possibly keep him company, it would be so nice? Of course he is a busy man, he will not take up much of your time, but it will be nice for him to have somebody to chat to over breakfast. The maids will have nothing to do whilst I am away, so you can easily have every meal you want at home." I knew, of course, that it was just a charming way of offering me a home, and the directing hands of Harry and Hester were very noticeable. Naturally I accepted, and that is how I entered 52 Campden Hill Square, a lovely Georgian house in the heart of Kensington. My room on the top floor was large, with a window to the back overlooking the little walled garden, and another window to the front overlooking the Square which also had a little garden in its centre. A big gas fire provided comfortable warmth.

I regularly had breakfast with Harry Fletcher and we always seemed to have plenty to talk about. Lunch I usually had on my own, in the evening I was mostly out, but very occasionally we had an evening meal together, and once or twice Harry took me to the theatre.

Hester Colles and Anna Coltman.

On several Sundays Harry took me to a little country house he owned in Hertfordshire named "Fiddler's Croft" because a violin maker had lived there in the seventeenth century. Originally three workmen's cottages, the place had undergone several changes and eventually been enlarged by the Fletchers. There was a charming garden, looked after very lovingly by a resident gardener-chauffeur and it was there that for the first time I drove a Vauxhall, a very elegant and immaculately maintained saloon car, of which, much later, I became the proud owner.

The weeks slipped by; I was due to go to Edinburgh for my first two examinations, and I knew that Mrs Fletcher was expected home during my absence. I had not yet had time to wonder where I would stay in Edinburgh, when Hester told me that I should get a letter from Lady Phillips inviting me to stay with her and Sir Robert. I was expected to accept. Sir Robert, I was told, was a famous doctor, a specialist in tuberculosis and the originator of the Scottish system of tuberculosis dispensaries which had been adopted by England. The invitation duly came and I accepted gratefully. However, before I went to Edinburgh Sir Robert was taken ill and the guest room was occupied by a resident nurse, but I was told he still expected me to be his guest, and that it had been arranged for me to be accommodated in a little guest house quite close to him.

84

Before I left Campden Hill I asked Mr Fletcher whether I could leave my things packed in his house until my return, as I was not quite certain where I would live next. "You leave everything where it is. Now that we have made friends my wife would be so disappointed if she did not get to know you more closely as well. We cannot keep you much longer because we are expecting visitors from the U.S.A., but anyhow, come back to us first."

Thus I travelled to Edinburgh, found the little guest house and was unpacking when the landlady came and said: "A gentleman to see you." With some surprise I went downstairs to meet my visitor. "I am Bruce Dick" he said, "Surgical assistant to Sir Robert. He is improving and expects us for tea tomorrow, but he tells me that you want to know something about the examinations here and that I should tell you in the meantime. Come with me, this place isn't licensed, we had better discuss matters over a drink." And so we went out and discussed examination techniques over a "wee dram". It was all new to me, I had never had to do written papers and the only knowledge I had of making pharmaceutical preparations myself was what I had learned in the practical course I had recently attended.

Next afternoon, at teatime, Bruce Dick picked me up. I had meanwhile discovered that he was a very well known chest surgeon himself, though he only stressed to me his position as assistant to Sir Robert.

There was a warm welcome at Sir Robert's. He was an old man, sitting in an armchair and evidently not well, but lively in conversation and showing much interest in my past and my plans. He pointed to a rhododendron in the corner of the room, full of bloom. "What do you think of it?" he asked — "how long might it have bloomed?" he persevered. "Are the blooms artificial?" I asked, a little hesitantly, as I had never before come across a rhododendron with artificial blooms. Sir Robert nodded approvingly. "You will pass your exams alright," he said with a smile.

I did pass my exams alright. There was no difficulty about pathology of which I had some knowledge as former demonstrator at the Vienna University, and I had had plenty of time in Switzerland to refresh my memory and brush up my knowledge. In pharmacology I just scraped by, but anyway I got my pass mark.

"You were very good, both of you," Hester praised us, "You will get an invitation from Mrs Benthall to spend Christmas together with your family in her house." We had a good time together and I was able to see something of Devon, with Magda driving Mrs Benthall's car under the supervision of the chauffeur; she had passed her driving test in Switzerland, but not in England, and Mrs Benthall did not trust her on her own with her precious Rover.

"You must visit Buckfast Abbey," I was instructed. It was quite near by car and I was very happy to have the opportunity, as I had heard of it before, and had an introduction from Professor von Hildebrand to Abbot Vonier. They knew each other well from the annual university summer school in Salzburg. When we arrived, and I asked for Abbot Vonier, I was told he had died a few days earlier, and had been buried the previous day. Not reading English newspapers at the time, I had not known. However, we were introduced to Father Mellitus, the senior monk of the Abbey, who told us something of its history. It had been re-erected on the site of an old pre-Reformation Cistercian monastery. The rebuilding had taken thirty years, Abbot Vonier being the inspiration and driving force behind it; having returned from a journey a few days previously, he had seen the Abbey for the first and only time without scaffolding. A few days later he was dead. The Abbey had been populated by monks from La Pierre-qui-Vire in France when they had to leave the country under an edict of the French Government, and many of the monks — including Father Mellitus — were German. We told him that for many years we had felt a special affinity with the Benedictine Order, and he there and then, in his capacity as Director of Oblates, accepted us as postulant oblates. About four months later, on St Mark's Day, April 25th, I was accepted in London as a full Oblate, and ever since I have visited Buckfast whenever possible and kept in close touch.

As soon as I had passed my first two examinations, I got in touch with the Refugee Committee to ask for allocation to a medical school and was referred to King's College Hospital. When I reported to Hester and Harry, and told them I was intending to go next day to see the secretary of the Medical School, they advised me to wait a day or two. Though a very good hospital, they said it was not the one for me, I should go to Westminster. How could I, having received my orders from the Committee? "Ask for an interview with the Dean," was the reply.

I do not think that a son was ever as willingly obedient to his parents as I to Harry and Hester; they always seemed to be right. I made an appointment to see the Dean of the Wesminster Hospital Medical School, which I got without delay, and so I went to his private consulting rooms in Portman Square. A butler opened the door and after a few minutes I was ushered into the presence of Sir Adolphe Abrahams, a famous consulting physician. We had a long and friendly interview, he appeared genuinely interested in what I had to say and, in the end, asked how about the fee. "There is an entrance fee of eight guineas and then a fee for each term." I seem to remember it was forty guineas each. "I have no money myself," I replied, "But I have no doubt that my friends will see to it that I can borrow what is necessary as I will never be able to make a living if I do not re-qualify for practice in this country." "If it was left to me I would admit all doctors from Austria," said the Dean, "But the trouble is I have only power to admit two. One vacancy is already filled and for the other you are the third applicant. Anyway, I shall write to you."

Three days later I had a handwritten letter from Sir Adolphe, saying he was pleased to tell me that I had been chosen to fill the second vacancy for a foreign doctor student at Westminster Medical School. His secretary was ill at the time, but that was no reason why I should not start at once. On his return the secretary would arrange with me all details. A few days later the secretary was back in the Medical School and sent for me to say that the Dean had asked if I could possibly pay the entrance fee of eight guineas, after which the Medical School would be happy to consider me as their guest.

Naturally I always felt indebted to my medical school and, consequently, when in later years I had my own practice, took Westminster Hospital students in their last year to live with us for 2 weeks at a time, showing them work in general practice. One of my first pupils was Ian Gregg, who later became very well known as a general practitioner who took special interest in asthma. In spite of his considerable achievements in that field, combining practice and research, he never gave up general medical practice. Some years ago he came as a guest speaker to our Medway Postgraduate Medical Centre, and on this occasion emphasised that the fact that he had remained in general practice was due to the enthusiasm instilled in him by me. Soon afterwards I was invited to accept election as a Fellow of the Royal College of General Practitioners – I had been a member since its beginnings – and I have always suspected that he had set the ball rolling.

In the meantime, I was back in the Fletcher house in Campden Hill Square, and Mrs Fletcher had returned from the U.S.A. My stay then was only short, but during those days our friendship was cemented and I was taken into the family and the everyday life of a comfortable and happy pre-war, cultured household. There were many friends coming to the house, and on some evenings music was made, particularly on the harpsichord which was a favourite instrument of the Fletchers.

Soon came the time when I had to leave because relatives were expected from America, but I was still a frequent visitor to the house.

I had not to worry where to live next. In good time I was told by the Colles that arrangements had been made. I am not now quite certain how it came about that a couple with whom they were friends and who happened to be neighbours of Anna Coltman, would not be using their flat for about two months, I believe they were to travel abroad. Anyway, I was back in Swan Court, in a slightly larger flat than Anna's, which I was to share with a young Austrian doctor who was also a refugee. Unfortunately he was not among the number of those admitted for studies in Britain, but he managed later to be admitted to Newfoundland, married there and ultimately had a flourishing practice in Canada. We corresponded for many years, and some years ago his son came over and visited us.

Eric Wermouth and I got on very well together. He was younger than I, handier than I, and, of course, had time on his hands. It was, therefore, he who prepared our daily breakfast and sometimes we had an evening meal together, though we usually were both invited out. Lunch I had at the Westminster Hospital.

Chapter 9
STUDENT AGAIN

I quickly settled in there. To be on equal terms with the young students made me feel young again, but on the other hand I also made more contact than is usual with the lecturers, in particular Mr Mullally, the senior surgeon, Dr Pulvertaft, the chief pathologist, Mr Hobart, the chief pharmacist, Dr Dudley Hart, then medical registrar, and Mr D'Abreu, one of the surgical registrars. Mr Mullally especially took me under his wing, and gave me much valuable advice. With Mr Hobart I had many pleasant games of chess, and I was particularly impressed by the fact that he always had time, always looked as if he had just stepped out of a bath, and, at the same time was known to be one of the busiest men in the hospital. Dr Dudley Hart, who has now retired as the senior consultant physician of the hospital, and I became very good friends, and our families visited each other for a long time after I had left the hospital.

From the students I experienced nothing but help and friendliness, and I had many pleasant hours with them in the Students' Club. I remember four particularly: Mr Gareth, who appeared to be a little older than the average; a young man called Llewellyn, who singled me out, so he said, because I was the only one to pronounce his name correctly ("Do you notice the horrible noise all the others make when they try to pronounce my name?" he used to say); Charles Drew, who later became a well-known thoracic surgeon, and John Wyman, who later became a consultant anaesthetist and Dean of Westminster Medical School. I started this, my second student time, in the old Westminster Hospital, but moved with them into the new building a few months before the outbreak of the second world war.

During the hospital year I went to Glasgow to sit my examinations in forensic medicine and public health. I received an invitation — in retrospect I feel tempted to say "of course" — from friends of the Colles to stay with them. They were Mrs Downie, a widow, and her daughter, a journalist, who lived in a very pleasant part of Glasgow. As always, I was very fortunate in having the ground prepared for me by Harry and Hester. I was accepted like a member of the family, and our friendship lasted. Mrs Downie is dead now, but Alison and we still correspond, and in spite of the great distance have occasionally met since.

I worked hard for the examinations, passed them without major difficulty, and returned to London to resume my student's year at Westminster.

In February Mrs Benthall fell ill, and could not keep Magda and our daughter Gabriele any longer in the house. Gabriele had all the time been for the mornings in the Teignmouth Convent of Notre Dame, in a nursery class. Now all the well laid plans seemed to have been upset. By that time I should have known better than to worry. As an immediate neighbour of Anna Coltman, I had, of course, seen a lot of her during my stay in the flat next door. She and the Colles knew the problem even before I did, and immediate help was at hand. Anna said she would travel to Teignmouth and sort matters out for us. She did so at once, and asked the Sisters at the Convent whether they were prepared to take Gabriele, in spite of her young age, as a full-time boarder; she would be responsible for the fees. The Sisters said they would take Gabriele, but declined the fees. "It will be our responsibility," they insisted, "and Gabriele will be our welcome guest until such time as doctor can pay something towards the fees." Thus, Gabriele became the youngest pupil ever at the Convent of Notre Dame and, staying during her whole school life, felt she really belonged there. She was extremely happy during all the years, being the pet of the Sisters, though she never felt estranged from her family. Of course she spent all holidays at home, as soon as we had a home. My wife was temporarily placed, by Anna, in a guest house in Teignmouth.

Just before Easter, when the McLarens were expected to return and need their flat, the Colles told me of yet another "invitation", this time from an old lady who would have liked to invite me to her home, but had no suitable accommodation, and consequently wished to remain anonymous. I was to stay, as her guest, in a little guest house in Oakley Street, Chelsea, where I found a small but comfortable room and a very friendly welcome from the landlady. As my things did not fit in the wardrobe provided in the room, additional space was made for me in a wardrobe on the landing for the overflow.

My life went on much as before, except that with the hospital taking up quite a bit of my time, I now often studied late in the evening, and was given, by the Colles, a little Melior coffee pot so that I could brew my own coffee and stay awake.

One day, soon after I had arrived at the guest house, the Reverend Ralph Sadlier called on me saying he had been sent by the Colles who were friends and parishioners of his. He was in charge of the "Old Church" Chelsea. He asked if I had met my parish priest yet, and when I replied that I had not, he said: "He's a friend of mine, I shall ask him to call on you." A day or two later Father Valentine called, gave me a warm welcome, and made me feel really at home in the parish.

Meanwhile, Mr Sadlier and I saw increasingly more of each other and were soon on Christian name terms and real friends. He explained that one of his ancestors, Sir Ralph Sadlier, had been jailer to Mary, Queen of Scots "but very kind to her". In his church the body of Sir Thomas More was buried, a fact of which he seemed very proud, and did not mind that he had died a martyr in defence of the Catholic faith, against the demands of the Church of England. The Colles were members of the Church of England, "Catholics of course," Hester said one day, "We are happy heretics, we recognise the Catholic Church even if the Church doesn't recognise us." The Fletchers also were Church of England, "Protestants of course". In Austria, the Catholic population was in the overwhelming majority, but there never seemed to be hostility between the various Christian churches, and it was only in England that I got to know of

89

anti-Catholic and anti-Protestant attitudes. With the background I have just explained, it is small wonder that this struck me as very strange. Of course I felt ecumenical all the time, and when ecumenism became the accepted policy of the Churches and gained popularity, I was more than prepared for it.

It was during the time of my stay at the Oakley Street guest house that my wife got an invitation to stay with Ralph Sadlier's parents at the Rectory in Coffinswell, Devon. Old Mr Sadlier was not in very good health, but was still active, in charge of Coffinswell and also a second parish, and he and his wife were extremely kind to Magda. It was then that she also met Ralph, when he went to visit his parents, and his younger brother Frank, who sadly was later killed in the war.

Time passed quickly, summer came and once more we were told that we had been very good (!) and it was now time that we had a family holiday together. The Colles had three invitations for us for one week each. First we went to Coltishall where we were the guests of Lady Maud Erskine in her lovely old manor house. We were given a tremendous bedroom, with an adjoining dressing room, my study was a drawing room with brocade-covered gilt antique furniture, and once again I experienced all the luxuries of a rich man without worries, with the added privilege of a charming hostess.

The next week we spent with teacher friends of hers, two spinster sisters who lived nearby in Little Hautbois. Their home was a tiny bungalow, but it had a little guest room. As a study they had pitched a tent for me in the middle of their lawn, so that I should be undisturbed. There was no electricity or gas in the bungalow, the lighting was by portable oil lamps, and I do not know with what they cooked, but their food was excellent and their kindness and hospitality quite out of this world. They had a little Hillman Minx and we were driven around and shown quite a bit of Norfolk and the Broads.

Our next stop was a guest house in Bridgewater, our host and hostess anonymous to us. We arrived on September 2nd 1939. The next day war broke out, and suddenly, to officialdom, we had become enemy aliens, subject to curfew and the limitation of movement to a radius of three miles. For me it lasted only about a couple of days, because I got a telegram from Westminster Hospital in which I, like all other students, was requested to report to the hospital for rescue training and emergency service. Magda and our little daughter stayed behind for a few days more, then Gabriele was able to return to the Teignmouth Convent. Old Mr Sadlier was ill at the time, so Magda could not return to there, but instead, again by an anonymous host, was settled into a guest house in Buckfast, close to the Abbey, where the restrictions of movement did not really affect her. I was back in the Oakley Street guest house and the hospital. In both places the daily routine had changed considerably.

There were many air-raid warnings at the beginning of the war, and though there was no bombing, it drove all the guests in the house to the basement. That is how, for the first time, I met and talked to some of them. Up to then we had only exchanged occasional greetings on the stairs. One of the ladies in the house,

The Rev Ralph Sadleir with Sue, who became later his wife.

Mrs Carol Leahy, introduced me to Chesterton by giving me her copy of "The Thing" which formed the beginning of a fairly large collection of Chesterton's works which I now have in my library.

In the hospital there were two events in those days which remain vivid in my memory. One was an air-raid exercise. The secretary of the Medical School and I had both volunteered as casualties, and were lying next to each other on stretchers in the open air waiting for attention. The exercise evidently did not go too well, because time passed and we got colder and colder without being collected. I probably would not have dared on my own, but lying next to the secretary we confided in each other that we had reached the limit of our endurance, and would probably become real casualties of the weather if we waited much longer. Thus, in the end, we took up our beds and walked into the entrance hall, still with our casualty labels round our necks, and reported to the Duty Officer as having rescued ourselves!

The other event was the setting up of a blood grouping service for transfusion purposes. Having had many years experience of laboratory work I suggested a minor modification in our technique to speed up the procedure. I cannot now remember what it was but it was enthusiastically approved by Professor Pulvertaft, who directed our volunteer group, and in the end he patted us all on the back by saying he thought the British with the help of the Austrians had done a very good job.

It was the end of October when Ralph Sadlier told me that the young curate and his wife, who had been staying with him, had now got their own home. He had meanwhile become so used to family life (he was a bachelor then) that he would very much like Magda and me to move in with him. Did I think Magda would be willing to come from the country and keep house for the four of us?, the fourth being Eric Wermouth with whom I had previously shared a flat in Swan Court. I cannot now remember if Eric went to live with Ralph Sadlier right away on leaving Swan Court, or came to him at the same time as we. Anyway, it was the same as always, the matter being put as if we did Ralph a favour whilst it was quite obvious that he gave us a home and a very good and comfortable home too. More — it was a happy home.

Many a morning we left the house together, Ralph going to hold a service in his church and I visiting mine, and many evenings we had long chats, occasionally involving theological questions. I well remember one evening Ralph saying to me with a naughty grin: "Now Kary, be careful, if you persuade me and thereby rob me of a job, I shall want to come and live with Magda and you."

There was actually a fifth member of our household, a little kitten called Tiddles, who had the habit of straying to one or other of two nearby pubs. Ralph used to take him on his knee and lecture him that this was not the right behaviour for "sons of the clergy" and that when Ralph himself had been a little kitten he never strayed to pubs.

For the Christmas holidays our young daughter joined us, but immediately afterwards I had to go to Edinburgh for my final examinations. This time I actually rented a room myself but as I had saved more than enough money, I was able to do so. The landlady was very kind and looked after me well, but unfortunately the fireplace in the room meant for me was unuseable, and instead I was given the huge dining room with a bed in it. January 1940 was a bitterly cold month, and the little fireplace in the large room was not really sufficient. I felt very much like Disney's dog Pluto, who, sitting in front of a fire, got pink in the front whilst blue in the back, and then turned round to get his back pink whilst the front turned blue! With me it was much the same except that it was right and left sides, with two armchairs in front of the fireplace, one to the right and one to the left on which I sat alternately. I attended final tutorials but for hours on end sat studying in my room, often joined by my wife's cousin, Dr Josephine Stross, who was to take her examinations at about the same time.

Work for the examinations was hard because foreign doctors had to sit the same papers and were marked in the same way as all the young students. There was only one among the examiners, Professor Johnstone, who treated me as an adult doctor, and that was in the oral examination in obstetrics. "Look as this case doctor," he said, "and tell me what you think of it. None of us is quite sure and we would like to discuss it with you and would value your opinion."

As if to make up for it, the oral examination in medicine was a nightmare. When I was allocated to a ward to examine a patient, a young student next to me, who had been sent to the same ward, said: "Good heavens. Goodall again, he has ploughed me once already."

Professor Goodall was an eminent physician, but had the reputation of being a very difficult examiner. Still, I was confident that in the practical examination I should not have any difficulties. What a mistake I made! Professor Goodall arrived one and a half hours late, which was not very good for my nerves, confident as I had originally been. "What is this man suffering from?" he asked me. "He complains . . ." I started off, in the knowledge that every doctor has to give a diagnosis based on the medical history. "Never mind what he complains of, what is he suffering from?" was Goodall's sharp reply. "He is suffering from arthritis, I believe it is rheumatoid but one would have to exclude a specific cause," I answered, trying to avoid the term "venereal disease" in front of the patient. "What do you mean by specific?" Goodall retorted. "Well he is complaining of urinary symptoms," I replied hesitatingly. "Oh, you mean he is suffering from gonorrhoea," the examiner blurted out to my discomfiture. "I don't think so, but feel it has to be excluded," was my somewhat dismayed reply. Professor Goodall wandered off without a word, went to another bed and waved me on. "Listen to this heart," he said. "What are you complaining of?" was my first question to the patient, having recovered my doctor-attitude. "I asked you to listen, not to ask questions," Goodall almost hissed. I listened and said as firmly as I could: "I do not hear any murmurs." In my own mind I realised that, even if there had been any murmurs, I probably would not have heard them as, at that stage, the only thing I would have heard would have been the rushing of my own blood! "Oh, it's a normal heart is it?" came the ironic question. "I didn't say anything of the sort" — I was furious as well as nervous at that stage — "There are plenty of heart complaints in which one doesn't hear murmurs." Again Goodall walked off without a word, took a test tube with urine from a stand and handed it to me as I stood in front of the bed. "What is that?" he asked. I shook the tube to see if it contained any sediment, and in my nervousness shook it too hard. A drop spilled over and fell on to an X-ray film which was lying on the bed, ready for me to look at and to diagnose. "That's because you always do things you are not told to do. Go away before you make more of a mess," he snarled at me. I hesitated. "Go away," he repeated. "I haven't been examined by the second examiner yet," I demurred. "I told you to go, there's the door," he almost shouted, pointing his finger at the door.

What could I do? Crestfallen, I slunk out of the hospital. After all that I could have no doubt that I had failed, which did not improve my spirits for the remaining examinations. Of course I also felt awful when, by telephone, I reported to the Colles: 'I am afraid I have failed in medicine."

It was only on the day before the results were announced that I happened to run into the student who had been examined in the same ward as I. To his question: "How are you?" I replied: "Not very happy." "Why not?" "Goodall ploughed me." "He didn't." "Of course he did, he threw me out." "But he didn't plough you," the student insisted. "What do you know about it?" I asked. "Well, when you left the hall, the other examiner came up to Goodall and said: "I haven't examined him yet." "Never mind," was Goodall's reply, "Let him go, he was quite good, as a matter of fact he was very good."

I couldn't believe my ears, but the next day it transpired that my information was right. I had passed, and on February 2nd 1940 received my Diploma of the Scottish Triple qualification.

When I reported to the Colles that I had passed they were surprised. It turned out that I had fallen into one of the famous language traps for foreigners. The story is told that one, arriving at a railway station, was told by the guard: 'I'm afraid you are too late and the train has gone," whereupon he started running to catch it, understanding that the guard had expressed a fear and not a fact. Similarly, when I had feared as a result of the examination just described, that that would mean the end of my hopes, I reported: "I am afraid I have failed," which the Colles interpreted as a fact.

Chapter 10
DOCTOR AGAIN AND INTERNMENT

When I left for my examinations in Edinburgh the household in Glebe Place broke up, Ralph Sadlier entering the Royal Navy as chaplain, Magda going to stay with her friend Johanna Breitenfeld in Hampstead, and I returned to the guest house in Oakley Street, where I had lived before. Of course my first concern was to get a job as assistant to a general practitioner, preferably with a view to partnership. Almost simultaneously I heard of a job with Dr Norman Porterfield of Rainham, Kent, through the medical agency of the British Medical Association and — through a monk friend of mine at Downside Abbey — of an opening with a doctor in Frome. I went first to Rainham and arrived there on a miserable March day, with the last of the snow melting, when the railway station and village looked at their worst. It did not look at all inviting, and it was in sharp contrast when a bright and smiling young thing, wearing an apron of green shot silk, opened the door to me at Dr Porterfield's house. I was very surprised when I discovered she was Dr Porterfield's wife! She showed me into their sitting room and said her husband would not be a few minutes — he was actually in the army, and stationed at Rochester, still looking after the practice part-time. It was not many minutes before he arrived and he too was very kind, seemed to like me, and the only disappointment was that when I started to tell him of my medical record he just said: "I'm sure you did everything that was needed." My pride was frustrated!

There was no difficulty about coming to an agreement, but I felt that I had to see the doctor in Frome, as Dom Leander of Downside had made the appointment for me to go there the next day. I explained this to Dr Porterfield, and he said: "Alright, go there, I'll keep open the job for three days, pending your decision."

The next day saw me in Frome. It was a dear, elderly doctor who offered me the job as assistant, but very kindly gave me a warning that he was not a healthy man, and that if anything happened to him I was unlikely, as an alien, to inherit his government appointments which represented about half his income. Moreover, he had an assistant at the time, but he was taking drugs and the principal wanted him to leave. Though I had really hoped to find something in the West Country to be near our daughter's school, I had to decline the job. I explained that the present assistant, if dismissed, would not blame his own drug taking, but be indignant that a foreign doctor — given hospitality in this country — was taking an English doctor's job. Thus we parted to our mutual regret.

Back in London, I rang Dr Porterfield's and it was his wife who answered the telephone. When I said I would like the job, she replied she thought I would, and she had meanwhile looked for accommodation for Magda and myself. "When will you come with your wife to see it?", she asked. We went the following day.

The accommodation was ideal. A big bedroom and sitting room in a spacious bungalow in Pump Lane, set in a large garden. There was a guest room which we could rent for school holidays; bathroom and dining room were, in theory, to be shared with the owner. However, they did not like any longer to live in that corner of the country which, by then, had become the route to London for the enemy raiders who, on occasion, dropped some unused bombs on their return flights. Consequently, they were leaving and, in practice, we had the bungalow to ourselves. We settled in, and I started work on March 8th, 1940.

I was supposed to have my own car for which I was to be given an annual expense allowance. Obviously, I could not afford to buy a car, but as always, help was at hand. Ralph Sadlier lent me his "for the time being" — pretending that it was better for the car to be kept in use by me than to lay it up until his release from the navy. It was a little 1934 Ford 8, of an elegance which in later years one did not usually associate with a Ford 8. A coach built two-seater, black with green coach lines, and the loveliest green leather upholstery. The Colles looked over it and decided that for my job I would need a fog lamp and trafficator arms, so that signals could be seen when I was on night calls. So those were fitted, and the car overhauled before it was handed over to me.

Dr Porterfield and I got on very well. He gave me complete freedom to run the practice as I thought fit, and told me that his wife Ngaire would help me with anything I needed.

We dispensed our own medicines, and that was something I had never done before. It was made comparatively easy by having stock solutions which were mostly ordered from a firm that specialised in preparing and labelling them with instructions with regard to diluting to make them up to the required strength. However, this did not apply to all the medicines dispensed, and we had to be very careful. Though Ngaire was used to it, having done the mixing under Dr Porterfield's guidance for a long time, I felt in conscience bound to check her work — but I never found her to make a mistake. Ngaire was also to deal with all the administration, and I should hand over any cash takings to her. This I did, keeping the money received in a separate pocket until — usually after surgery hours — I could empty the pocket out on to her desk. My takings were never queried, and I felt that I had their full trust. As Dr Porterfield was still in the army, and stationed nearby, he occasionally gave me a hand.

Work was hard I suppose, but I enjoyed it. Probably it was the fact that I had been faced with doubt if I would ever be able to practice medicine again which made me extra enthusiastic, so that I did not mind the long hours. For me, this time is still the "good old days" though many doctors today would consider it the bad old days. Patients had no cars or no petrol then, and any day on which I did less than twenty visits seemed easy to me. The visits led far out into the country, because Dr Porterfield was what was then known as "the parish doctor" of several surrounding villages. This meant that any poor of the parish could get a card from the vicar which entitled him or her to medical attention and medicine

Dr Norman Porterfield.

Ngaire Porterfield.

from the parish doctor or from his deputy, for which a yearly fee was paid by the parish. Quite often on the visits the doctor had to deal with situations which no longer arise; because ambulances were not radio-controlled they often could not be got quickly. Also patients were loath to go into hospital because they felt that, in the case of an air-raid, they would be safer with the family. Again, in illnesses like pneumonia, numerous return visits were often necessary before the age of the various anti-biotics. Catheterisation, in the case of complete urine retention, had frequently to be carried out in very primitive surroundings; the same applied to child-birth which, in those days, was almost completely domiciliary.

The joy of work was all too short lived. It was on Whit Sunday, May 12th, 1940, when I had just returned from Mass, that D.C. Coe called and said that he had to take me to an interview. Though I had already passed the Tribunal, all men living in the South East of England were to be screened again; because France was struggling for survival, an invasion of Britain had become a possibility, and no risks could be taken that enemy aliens might help the invaders. When I asked what I should take with me in case I was detained for any length of time, D.C. Coe said I might take, for safety, a spare shirt and a pair of pyjamas, but he did not really expect this would be necessary.

I was taken to the West Kent Barracks in Maidstone, and there it transpired that Coe had been wrong. There was no question of an interview then; we were all detained to be moved after a day or two to a camp in Huyton. Interviews were to take place later on. I heard afterwards that D.C. Coe was taken by surprise, he had not expected it, and actually returned to comfort my wife. He later made a career up to chief inspector, and we became very friendly. In Huyton the basic difference in the German and the Austrian outlook on life became very obvious. The Germans were very serious, pessimistic and resentful; we Austrians — and we were eight in the small council house where we were accommodated — looked at the positive side. A patch of lawn in front of our little house was a cheering sight which we did not want to have trampled on, so we made a small brick wall around it from bricks we found lying about. However, next day they were required by the workmen elsewhere and taken away. We then found some wooden slats, and used them for fencing, but again they were required and taken away. We finished up with small pieces of wood which we fixed around the lawn in crossed shape, not really making a fence, but a boundary marking. "Disgusting; these Austrians just behave as if they enjoyed themselves here," a passing German internee was heard to say.

We did not enjoy ourselves, but we understood the reasons for our internment, and felt we should make the best of it, for ourselves as well as for the country. I shared a little box room with an internationally known aircraft designer, Hafner by name. He had worked for the Ministry of Aircraft Production, and had a British wife and British-born daughter. We each had a palliasse on the bare floor on opposite sides of the room as the only furniture. The middle of the room, though small, looked depressingly bare, so we begged a bit of camouflage paint from the workmen in the camp, and painted a sort of carpet square to cheer ourselves up. Much later, when I had returned to Rainham, I told one of our midwives about this, and much later still she told me of a strange coincidence. Our camp had afterwards been used by the army, and a nephew of hers was stationed there. He told his aunt: "Fancy, somebody painted a carpet in the box room. I wonder who that was?", to which his aunt replied: "I can tell you exactly," and told him my story.

Two men from the Ministry of Aircraft Production came to see Hafner and brought him cigarettes and chocolates, the latter of which I shared. They urgently wanted him released but had been told that no relevant regulations had yet been issued by the Home Office. They proposed to furnish him with a drawing office in the camp if he would be willing to continue his designs. He asked my advice, saying he feared that if he consented he might never be released because his freedom would be of no use if he was not again given entry to airfields, which at that time seemed somewhat doubtful. However, he agreed with me that everything possible should be done to help Britain's war effort, and he therefore consented to continue work in the camp for a limited time. I did not witness the outcome because, before this, most internees were transferred to Douglas, Isle of Man. Many saw this as the end of the road, and one German doctor — who practised near me in Gillingham — said: "Once the water is between us and the mainland we shall never get out." He struggled to stay behind in Huyton, and succeeded, but I was released and returned to Kent long before him.

One hardship in the first days of our internment was that we could not communicate with home. No letter could reach us and we could not write, because our letters had to be censored and no censor had yet been appointed. To make up for this I wrote a kind of diary for my wife — then still in German — from which I here quote, translated into English, the parts which will give a picture of our life and thoughts in those days. I started off the notes in letter form:—

"Now our joint life had to be interrupted once again and it all came a bit suddenly, but I should say this is better than if one could have seen it coming. It would only have caused a heavy heart and in many words and many hours we would not have been able to say more to each other than in this sudden goodbye.

"And so I am once again in a new world and it gives insight into life from a different angle. There are many, many new impressions and it is difficult to collect and recount them. Every postal communication is at present forbidden so I thought I might write this sort of diary for you and hope I can take it with me on my release . . . We were the first instalment to arrive in Maidstone comprising about twelve people from Gillingham and neighbourhood, but soon other groups came, and I think we are now eighty-nine, a motley crowd. Dr Wolpert from Gillingham, a house physician from St Bartholomew's Hospital, a German doctor who had served in India for a few years, an ear specialist and another German doctor about whom I do not know much. These are the medical people. Among the others is one priest from Germany, pale and quiet, who worked in one of the local churches and whilst we were very glad to have a priest among us he does not seem to participate in that joy!

"There are some youngsters, only just 16, who were put on a farm to learn agriculture by a Zionist organisation. Some of them have a mandolin and from time to time they sing melancholy Hebrew airs which are reminiscent of Russian tunes. Then there are a few elderly men. We live here in Maidstone on a big shooting range and camp like the soldiers. Palliasse next to palliasse. In front of the house in the open are long trestle tables. a few pails and basins made of tin, water comes to us through a hose which is connected in the kitchen for us, at times we even get warm water. Round the corner behind canvas is a lavatory installation. Everything of course is very improvised, and we are very fortunate in having beautiful weather. I cannot imagine what we would do in rain, where we would wash and where we would live. The officers have almost apologised to us and have said that it is only provisional accommodation and they do for us whatever is possible, whatever they have themselves they share with us.

"They have put at our disposal an unused lawn tennis court; according to regulations we can use it for four hours and during meals, but as it is so hot they always leave us in the open much longer. The lieutenant in charge of us is a particularly fine, quiet man and looks like somebody out of a picture book. I am sure our little Gabriele (our daughter: aged 6) would be completely in love with him and I am sure he is very nice to children. Actually he is very nice to us even though, of course, the circumstances which are characterised by the barbed wire and the guards force a separation between us. But across this I seem to feel his particular sympathy and I hope he feels mine, though of course I never approach him. But he uses me sometimes for little bits of information as interpreter. At first he knew me just as the Austrian doctor, now he has managed to learn my name.

"Now back to our life. The main thing seems to be the meals. Food is fantastically ample and good. Breakfast about 9 a.m., after we have got up at 6 a.m. and had roll call at 7, and then had a wash, which takes a long time because there are far too few basins. Here are sample menus: Yesterday for breakfast, porridge, fried egg and chips, tea, white bread, margarine and marmalade. Today a similar breakfast but instead of the chips, two eggs. At 11 o'clock morning break consisting of cocoa and biscuits, at 1.30 lunch, ample meat (today very good goulash) with two vegetables and a pudding. Everything is very well cooked. For tea yesterday bread, egg and jam, today a cake, bread and jam. Evening meal at 7 o'clock, again very good but yesterday I was unable to eat it, I only drank a cup of cocoa. After all one cannot fatten oneself to that extent eating full military rations whilst one does not work at all. We walk up and down the tennis court, then walk round it, lie in the sun and look at the parade ground next door where the soldiers are trained. It looks like sport and games, but we know that over the whole of Europe it is in bitter earnest. It can mean death any day for these young people who guard us today, feed us, bring us books and shop for us at Woolworths for little necessities like a mirror, shoe polish or hand towels. Every day the corporal in charge accepts a long list of things we need and accounts for his expenses to the penny. And during all this time they need doctors on the battlefield. Dr Porterfield must work very hard and probably already looks for another assistant whom he will probably get without difficulty, and who, I am sure, will not be as happy in his job as I was. And I am here doing nothing. Just the same, whilst I have longing thoughts and feel ashamed to be so useless, I know that I would prefer a much harder life if by it I could help anybody, help the suffering people and help this country which was and is so good to me. If only I could visibly stand with those who fight the beast that brings sadness to so many people. But as I am unable to do so I try to live according to the prayer that Father Leander taught me: "Never to look beyond me, out of my little sphere, if I could fill another, God would not keep me here." And I try to do God's will whilst I lead my life here quietly and almost cheerfully and give comfort to others whenever I can and am allowed to. I thank God for his guidance and use the time for reading, the daily Mass text and Father Baker's 'Holy Wisdom'. I must say that of all the people here I am probably the most fortunate, partly because of my faith, partly because I need have no worries knowing that you are cared for by the Porterfields, knowing that Hester cares and that I am prayed for. And so I have just to live according to what has always been my motto: 'It is not really important what happens to us, but important is only what we ourselves create out of anything sent to us.'

"Of course one wonders for how long we are stuck here, whether there is truth in the rumour that we are going to be transported to the Isle of Man and will that mean a long internment. When shall I be released and what shall I be allowed to do then? — and still, how small are such problems compared with those of innumerable people who, minute by minute, are robbed of their very existence, of all hope, faith and love by Hitler's hate and Hitler's bombs. Isn't it strange how all evil instincts can find their expression in one single man? He, so it seems, is actually a manifestation of the anti-Christ, the touch-stone for good and evil, like Christ was — but in reverse.

"The 'prince of this world' — today he seems to be triumphant, but how little will be needed to bring him down when God decides it is enough.

"My thoughts wander and in me are mixed feeling of sadness and comfort. On the shooting range the soldiers practice and on the parade ground two little girls play, one has a bunch of yellow flowers, the other rides a tricycle, and I think of our own little blonde girl. How sad it would be if she were told that her daddy is in internment and she would lose the feeling of being at home; but I hope the examination of our cases will start soon and then every-thing will come alright. On the other hand, when I shall be able to write to her that I am in a camp with many soldiers she will think I am working here as a doctor and will be happy . . . One of my neighbours on the palliasse is a particularly pleasant engineer from Vienna." (The aircraft designer mentioned before.)

"Conservatives, members of the Labour party and Zionists are all mixed up, but I have not yet met a Communist and I do not think there is any Nazi in disguise here, but of course he would be very careful not to show his true colours . . .

"It is a good experience for me, I think it is a reason for gratitude whenever we have the opportunity to look into other people's way of life. All the same I pray that it will not be too long before I shall be able to come home and help where I am needed, and bring children into this world for what we hope will be a more peaceful and happier life or to bring comfort to the dying or those who are recovering from severe illness.

"May 15th, 1940. Today was a very busy day. In the morning I washed my laundry with my own paws, and in the afternoon was bath time, rather a 'quickie' ten minutes for four people, but all the same one gets some feeling of cleanliness . . . the news of Holland is very disquieting but then the calm cheerfulness of the British soldiers acts as a comfort and nobody doubts for a moment that everything will turn out alright in the end and the Nazis will have a sudden and very thorough routing . . . According to the latest rumours we shall stay here until the end of the week and then go on to a camp to be sorted out, but nobody knows how soon this will take place. I wonder if Hester and Harry are already making attempts to hasten my case or if they have to give it up as impossible. Actually it is fortunate that the word 'imposs-ible' does not figure in Hester's vocabulary — but she might well feel that one cannot trouble the authorities at the moment with individual cases whilst bigger things are at stake. I myself have this feeling occasionally, but all the same I have the urge to get out, not for my pleasure but to be usefully occupied in these times when doctors are in such short supply. I will admit that also the wish to have my honour restored plays a part, which, after all, seems to be in doubt as long as I am here.

"16th. A day of laziness in the sunshine, and our moods up and down like the battle in France. We wait and hope that at last he is stopped and the fiction of the Fuehrer's God-given mission will come to an end . . .

"We lie in the grass, already quite sunburned, and the youngsters do gym and play ball as in a holiday camp, and whenever the ball flies beyond the barbed wire there is always one soldier who, with touching patience, returns it so that the play should not be interrupted . . . I feel that everything is so unreal, as a stage between dreaming and waking, and my thoughts seem to have as much substance as the real happenings around me. I do not talk to many people but read much of Father Baker's 'Holy Wisdom' and the daily missal. If Carl (Father Breitenfeld), Father Leander or Johannes were here I could make this a fruitful retreat, notwithstanding the upheaval around me. Our Father Haring does not seem to be able to detach himself from the daily happenings.

"17th. Now it is 5 o'clock in the evening and we are supposed to leave at 6.30. First stop Liverpool, what happens then is uncertain but there are rumours of the Isle of Man. Whatever happens, experience up to now shows that we will not be badly treated but what about you if the matter is prolonged? Will you be able to stay at the Porterfields, or will they want you to move out of Kent? . . . How good that the summer holidays are still far away, so possibly our little rabbit will not realise that her daddy, the 'British doctor', is still considered an alien here and be saddened by it . . .

"There is little to tell about the day. In the morning we wrote jointly a letter of thanks to Lieutenant Perkins, who was in charge of us here but was sent on a course. His successor is again a very nice and handsome young lieutenant who speaks German fairly fluently and whom I have met before, because the very first day I helped him to translate the camp roll. He will take us to Liverpool. The remainder of the day went by with reading, packing and basking in the sun." (Actually we were taken to Huyton.)

"Huyton, 19th. Now we have just to wait for the special writing paper which is the only one we shall be allowed to use, then we shall be able to write. Our life has changed very much since last I wrote. We live here in small houses like on a council estate, each house has eight to eleven inmates which means two people in each of three or four rooms and three people in the largest. We are very fortunate in our house. I share a small box-room with the engineer who was my palliasse neighbour in Maidstone. We have three more young people, two middle-aged and another man from Vienna. We have put a board up on the house giving it the name 'Old Vienna'. Our palliasses are on wooden frames, we have running cold water, electric light, black-out arrangements, a real lavatory — and peace. Yesterday a lot of guards were still about, but today they only watched the perimeter fencing around the camp and we can walk along the streets, the whole thing giving the impression of a Sunday afternoon in a small provincial town. But, of course, women and children are missing, and a church. I suppose some possibility for saying Mass will be created in a few days, we now have three priests in the camp (all from Germany), one Anglican clergyman and one Rabbi. We get meals in the canteen, all of good quality and pleasant, with six people to a table. Each house had to elect a leader (we chose to call him 'house-father') who discusses with the camp commander whatever is necessary. I was rather pleased that I was unanimously voted to do the job, not because I considered it an honour but as a sign that I was right in thinking that I am liked in spite of having kept myself so much to myself. Moreover, I am pleased that our house is an example of unity, a few occasions of irritation were quickly overcome. I act on the principles of the Benedictine Rule.

"The officers are charming, but with all the many people arriving (some came from Edinburgh today) it is impossible to say how long it will take until our further fate is decided. Also the censorship is not yet established and we have had no letters though we were told some had been forwarded from Maidstone. Meanwhile there is a lot of work to be done here. All in all we are now six doctors who requalified in Britain. We help the camp doctor, and for hours today examined new arrivals for infections and fitness to be kept in the camp; there is also a full examination of all the camp inmates, house by house. We shall have work for at least a week, and the fact that we can once again do our own work and be useful to this country is a comfort and helps to pass away the time. It is rather comical when sometimes one of the internees thinks we are influential persons, and is rather startled when he realises that we are fellow internees. And so the time passes, and if it were not for the sadness about the suffering of the people on the battlefield, and that the Germans have still successes, life here would not be too bad . . . and the very fact that we are now known by many and treated as doctors rather than prisoners gives one a feeling of anticipation that one day life will again be normal, and that Gabriele will be able once more to be proud of daddy, the 'British doctor.'

"26th May. Sunday again, and the week passed very quickly. Every night I am dead tired and sleep splendidly until the morning, as a result of the double and very ample duties, as father of the house and as a doctor. On the happy side there is the unity of our house and our constant endeavour to embellish it within the small scope at our disposal, and the feeling that one can help those who lose their nerve. On the sad side is the fact of how many do lose their nerve; it shows once more that man does not live by bread alone and here is nothing to nourish the majority of them but just the food. Of course it is hard to be without news from home, we ourselves shall now be allowed to write two letters of twenty-four lines a week. Still I shall continue my notes here a bit longer, because of the restricted opportunity to write letters. The fact that we have no news from home is aggravated by the fact that we are not allowed any newspapers.

". . . I meet a lot of people, some I have known for a long time, others only from hearsay. Some sixty doctors are now here, but still only six who have requalified and are entitled to practice.

"We have now arranged a little chapel for Sundays, it was crowded which made it very beautiful. On weekdays Mass is said in the room of our priest in my own 'Old Vienna' house. I am the only layman there as the room would not hold more. A small ship's altar is erected between the beds, everything is improvised but has its own charm if one thinks that it all started in the stable of Bethlehem.

"29th May. Hester's telegram today. How good she is and how good to know you are with the dear Fletchers and to be able to picture your surroundings. Now I can be at peace awaiting your letter though, of course, there are a lot of questions I would like answered. However, knowing you are in the care of the Colles, Fletchers, Anna and dear Johanna you are sure to be much better off than you would have been in Kent.

"Life is strange here without newspapers, with rumours all over the camp. They all say that the situation is grave but I always feel the same confidence of a successful outcome, and that the Nazi reign will crash. I retain faith in a better future, even here on earth . . .

"31st May. Today the expected parcel arrived but raised some questions in my mind. I missed your handwriting and also that among all the things only the nailfile and the handkerchiefs are of my own belongings. Does it mean that our belongings are still held back for search, or does it mean that there is some hope of my returning to Kent soon?

"The crowd in my house are really very good. We all look after the house with the very primitive means that we have, even if sometimes it is difficult. And as there is much less medical work now I help in the house. If you could have seen me today, washing walls and doors and the WC! I decided that hygiene is a matter for the doctor. There was also my laundry to be done. Then I sat in my room and read, partly in Father Baker's book, partly in a school book of English history covering the years 1485 to 1714. How good that we have such friends, I can almost see dear Mrs Fletcher thinking how to put together the parcel, can see her and Harry looking after and encouraging you, and surely also Hester and Harry (Colles), Anna (Coltman) and Ralph (Sadlier)."

A few days later we were transported to the Isle of Man and put into the central promenade camp in Douglas, which faced the sea, fenced off with barbed wire, and I estimated that it comprised about thirty houses, three of which provided kosher food for the orthodox Jews. I was allocated No. 3, a second-class boarding house, which had to take seventy-one internees. On each room door was written the number of internees to be accommodated therein with a corresponding number of bed places provided. However, a double bed was, in army launguage, accommodation for two people, so most men had to share a bed. While they all looked into every room before making up their minds, I ran up the stairs to the top and found an attic with two double beds, but which was meant to accommodate two people only, the limited air space not allowing for more. The one bed near the window was mine in the twinkling of an eye!

Each house was asked to appoint a leader and a deputy leader, but we explained to the British officers that we were rather sensitive to the word leader, and would prefer the title "house-father".

The crowd in my house elected me, and I told them I thought it was a good idea to see how the Germans would get on under Austrian guidance while Austria was evidently doing very badly under the German leadership. There was, however, one stipulation I made before accepting; the deputy house-father should not be elected but appointed by me. I explained that as far back as around 500 AD, St Benedict, who was a very wise man, stipulated that the prior — second in command of an abbey — should never be elected but be appointed by the abbot as otherwise there might be differing, or even opposing, policies. The same I felt applied to us. I had to be sure that my deputy would always act in the same spirit as I. To my surprise my ideas were accepted unanimously without any discussion, and I appointed Mr Pinchoff, another Austrian Catholic.

Among the internees in my house was an epileptic, a Bavarian artist, and I suggested that he should be given the second double bed in the attic which I occupied as I was probably the best person to deal with him in case he had a fit. This was generally approved. Another suggestion I made concerned a damp and dark basement room which had been officially allocated to four inmates. I felt sure that whoever lived in that room would be very dissatisfied and I said so, suggesting that we should rearrange beds in the other rooms. The basement room I said would be suitable only for one thing, to make it into an oratory for the Catholic internees in the camp and actually would be very suitable for this as the darkness would prevent the shabbiness of our equipment being shown up. This too was accepted without any objections, and having at the time seven priests in the camp this little make-shift chapel was very much used and was a great comfort to the Catholic inhabitants. I had, of course, first to get the permission of the British officers but they said they did not mind the rearrangement as long as I got 71 people accommodated in the house. In spite of my ideas, which must have seemed strange to some of the crowd who were a mixture of staunch church people of various denominations, young Zionist pioneers and unbelievers, I somehow managed to remain popular and I believe we were the most peaceful house in the whole camp. I always ascribed this to the oratory being in our house, where Mass was said every day and where often during the day one could find men, not only from our own house, kneeling in prayer. In the evenings we arranged for Benedictine Compline, led by our senior priest who was parish priest of Painswick and an Oblate of Prinknash Abbey, which he later entered to become a monk. I had sent to me from home a C.T.S. pamphlet containing Compline, which Father Sandkuhl — later Dom Clement — annotated for me to convert it into the Benedictine version. I still treasure it as a souvenir inscribed with a dedication by "my chaplain" as he used to call himself.

Of course I encountered a few difficult situations. Among the internees in our house were three miners from Scotland, who, as small children, had come with their parents to this country. They were particularly suspect because they had had the opportunity for a long time to be naturalised but did not claim their right. To me their reason was obvious — they did not want to spend the money which they thought would be wasted, as they never envisaged a situation in which their nationality mattered. Whenever there was any discussion in which German was spoken, they violently objected: "You and your bloody German." I solved the problem by proposing that the language at all official meetings should be English, not only for their sakes but also because we all intended to go on living in this country, and the more we got used to speaking English the better.

With young people in the house there had to be some mischief. At that time of the year the days were long but not long enough for them. They did not want to go to sleep when it became dark, but we had no black-out curtains and therefore were supposed to go to bed with the birds not to break the black-out regulations. My responsibility!

Of course I had "spies" out who told me that some of the youngsters read in bed, switching on lights, and I therefore made an evening round, finishing by disconnecting for safety the main switch. However, one adventurous youngster had an idea: wait until house-father is in bed, then creep down to the cellar to switch on the main switch again and read happily. He misjudged me. I was still young enough to anticipate his plan and left the switch on my own bed lamp in the "on" position, which gave me a warning. I had not long to wait — on came the light, giving me the signal that the deed had been done. In a flash I turned out my light, jumped out of bed, did bare-footed another round of inspection and took the culprit by surprise.

There was another temptation. Some of the best furniture and a few delicate things, among them a wireless receiver, had been stored away by the proprietors in a little box room which was secured with a padlock. We were anyway not allowed a wireless, though we were given news bulletins. Of course some of the young ones were dying to listen to the full news on the wireless. One day they forced the door of the box room and told me triumphantly of their exploit. Now we could hear the news without anyone knowing — "not me!" "Do you really think you can keep a secret of which 71 people know? Do you really think it is worthwhile to stay interned for the duration of the war for a few days' possession of a wireless?" I made my point. It remained for me to tactfully liquidate their adventure. I went to our welfare officer: "There was a little argument in the corridor, somebody was pushed and fell against the door which gave way. A wireless was found." A sergeant came with a big blanket to wrap up the set and carry it off. The door was secured again. No questions were asked: the obvious white lie was appreciated!

We had one internee among us who soon drew the hostility of all others upon himself. Though opposed to the Nazis, he was the type who believed: "right or wrong my country". He therefore wished for a German victory in the war and upbraided the other Germans for siding against their native country. I was exempted. "You are an Austrian and your Emperor died in exile. It is quite natural that you should feel as you do," he said. Though thus personally absolved by him, his attitude created for me many difficulties as house-father as he objected to practically every resolution a house meeting proposed. Knowing he was a religious man (Protestant), serious in his convictions, and at heart "anti-Nazi", I did not want to denounce him, but it became imperative to solve the problem. I therefore had a talk with him, in which I explained all this, adding that I did not want his opinions suppressed by others, but that he could not expect, with his lone voice, to upset the feeling in the house which otherwise was expressed unanimously. I consequently suggested that he should write down his own opinion which I would make sure the officers received together with the general meeting report. Obviously he had to accept this suggestion and within three days he was transferred to another camp, into which I hope he fitted better.

My position as house-father meant that I had fairly frequent dealings with the British officers who had their office outside our camp, which was surrounded by barbed wire, with guards patrolling outside. This led to the almost comical situation that whenever I wanted to go to the office I just summoned a guard who then patiently trotted behind me with fixed bayonet. Soon a relationship of trust developed between the officers and myself, particularly with a grey-haired lieutenant who was our welfare officer. He once told me that he was paying for the war out of his own pocket, because he really was a retired brigadier who had felt he wanted to do something useful in the war and joined up as an acting lieutenant, his pay as such being less than the pension of a brigadier which rested during his time of active service. He soon found out that in our camp there was nobody really suspect, and again he remarked to me one day: "I don't think we handled this internment very well, it is much easier to handle these things under a totalitarian regime. But I wouldn't like one because of that, would you?" I certainly would not.

Every evening for the night roll call I stood on the doorstep reporting: "71 all present and correct," and usually the duty officer came in and had a quick count, or at least a look round. Once it happened that Mr Smeed, the lieutenant I mentioned, supplying for others, was on duty three nights running. He came, accompanied by a sergeant, and I made my normal report. "Thank you," he said, "Goodnight," and walked by. The next night I made the same report. "You wouldn't tell me a lie would you?" he said, smiling at me, "Goodnight," and again walked by. The third night he evidently felt that he could not do that again, so he said: "I'll just go in and say goodnight to them," and so he did. After my release Mr Smeed and I still remained in contact by occasional correspondence, and my wife and I actually were twice invited to his house when we were in his neighbourhood.

107

All the time in Huyton, and for some time still in Douglas, we were completely cut off from home. Though we could write letters they could not be sent out because they had to be censored and no censor had yet been appointed. Of course we could not receive letters either, and actually I am not quite certain when the families first knew of our whereabouts. I therefore still existed with the one spare set of underwear and shirt I had brought with me, and it was lucky that it was a very good summer so that we could wash and have the laundry dry within a few hours. Bed linen was non-existent and we slept on the bare mattresses, but after a little while we could get the most essential things, and some books, sent from home.

It belonged to the house-father's task to organise the cleaning of house and yard, and arrange for the collection of rations, their cooking and distribution. Regarding the kitchen we were very fortunate in having a brother from a religious community who used to be cook in his monastery; he acted as chef and in consultation with him I arranged for his helpers. I never lacked volunteers for the necessary tasks. "I need so many volunteers for that and that," I would announce at breakfast. "I am one of them." And almost always the reply came: "We can't let the house-father do that," and there was always an extra volunteer. The only task I insisted on reserving for myself was keeping the lavatories clean as I thought others might be squeamish about that, and doctors are supposed not to be!

For conducting house meetings I was given a special gavel, an old croupier's hammer which one internee had found in a drawer and which was painted up for me and inscribed. I don't think I ever needed it to keep order, but I still have it in memory of those days.

I soon had a second task which usefully and agreeably occupied my time. The doctor in charge of the camp was the Medical Officer of Health for Douglas, who inspected the camp once a week. There were many old and ailing people among us, and we had four doctors who had qualified in Britain among the camp population. I therefore suggested to the official camp doctor that we would in turn man a daily out-patient clinic, and then when he came once a week show him any cases which we thought needed his attention, particularly regarding their fitness to remain in internment. He at once agreed and also that one of us should be on emergency night duty every night; he even took it upon himself to have the duty doctor issued with a torch. I still have a letter from him which he gave me on my release saying that both the patients and he had been extremely grateful for my "kindness and help". He had just retired as Medical Officer of Health when I met Dr McPherson again in May, 1973 at the Annual Police Surgeons Conference which that year was held in Douglas. He was among the visitors and we recognised each other and spoke of the old times.

The even flow of the days was rudely interrupted when the order came that all single people in the younger age group (I cannot now remember the exact age limits) were to be evacuated, some to Canada, some to Australia. Up to that time we had seven Catholic priests in the camp and they all fell into this category. However, I managed to persuade the officers that they should leave the senior priest with us, as I felt it was not right that we should be left without a chaplain.

Having from then on only one priest in the camp meant that we had only one Mass, even on Sundays, whilst up to then there were usually seven daily Masses celebrated. Consequently our oratory became too small for Sunday Mass and with the ready consent of the inhabitants, the sitting room was used. We also managed to borrow a harmonium from one of the orthodox Jewish houses, which by united efforts was carried to our house each Sunday and taken back when Mass had ended. The young people having had to leave meant that our camp now contained an ageing population which was to be supplemented with a similar population from other camps in the country. This posed a problem, because up to then the youngsters had usually been willing for a few pence pocket money to do some of the physically harder jobs for the older men, who mostly were able and very happy to pay small sums to be relieved of physical work they were unused to and therefore found hard.

The immediate problem, however, was to prepare for the new arrivals, which were to be sent from other camps to replenish our numbers. I was aware that they would be hungry, apprehensive and not very happy about the transfer into new surroundings, so I thought it imperative to give them a good welcome and some food. As we could not draw rations for them until they had actually arrived, I persuaded my flock to save some food from our own meagre rations in the hope that this would break the ice. There was some compensation for those who had stayed behind in being able to change rooms so that they could move in with friends they had made.

Things went more smoothly than I had anticipated. I looked at the newcomers, sorted them out in my mind, allocated them to the vacant beds — as I said before all double beds each for two men — without so much as by your leave. To my surprise no questions were asked. The explanation came much later. Soon we settled into a new routine and time passed; luckily it was one of the best summers on record.

Meanwhile, my friends were busy working for my release. Dr Porterfield pressed for the necessity of my reappointment as he was sure to be posted abroad before very long. Other friends with suitable connections urged review of my case at the Home Office, pointing out that I had already passed one tribunal. Archbishop David Mathew lent his support. The Fletchers, who had at once taken my wife in when she was left alone in Kent, offered accommodation for me if I could not be released back to Kent at once, Hester and Harry Colles, of course, were behind it all, mobilising the right people, and when on August 19th I was notified to be at the camp gate with my luggage the next morning ready for release to 52 Campden Hill Square, I was the first to leave our camp, and actually one of the first internees in the country to be released.

In the afternoon of my last day in camp I was given a formal farewell tea, not much food, but genuinely warm speeches. One of the latecomers said: "I don't know doctor if you will be pleased or offended by what I have to say, but I thought you should know that when the second group of internees arrived we had no idea that you were a fellow internee. We all thought you were a catering man put in by the government." Here then, at last, was the explanation of my unquestioned success the first evening.

Chapter 11
PRACTICE AS ASSISTANT

The journey was uneventful, and I was back in Campden Hill Square to a very wonderful and loving welcome. To return to Kent, special permission was needed from the War Office, the Home Office and the Chief Constable of Kent because of the proximity of Chatham Dockyard which demanded particular protection for that area, and it was not until late in October that the last of the hurdles was cleared. All that time my wife and I stayed with the Fletchers in Kensington. It was the period of the blitz on London. Mr Fletcher had converted one of the basement rooms into a relatively comfortable shelter. The ceiling of the room had been reinforced to take, if necessary, the weight of the whole house in case of a direct hit. There were three camp beds for the Fletchers and my wife. My own camp bed was just outside in the corridor which, because of the narrow span of the ceiling was no less safe. Apart from the night's sleep, I shared the shelter room where, on a big table, we had our regular evening meal. There was also, of course, a wireless and an electric tea kettle. In spite of austerity and improvisation, life was very civilised. After supper we sat together, Mrs Fletcher and Magda knitting, and it was then that I learned to knit, not to sit idle. Mr Fletcher read aloud to us, and I still remember some of "Dr Johnson's Life" and "The Hunting of the Snark". When the first warning sirens of the evening sounded, Mr Fletcher donned his warden's overall and steel helmet and off he went, being a regular warden in spite of his 70 years. By the way, he had arranged for my wife to help in the wardens' canteen during the day, in the night she was not allowed out because of the curfew. I myself would have loved to be of help, but my permit to stay was in Kensington, my permit to work, which had never been revoked, was for the Medway Towns only, so I had to stay – or sit – put to comply with the terms of the guarantee the Fletchers had given. With houses bombed all over and around Campden Hill, when I could have done useful work as a doctor, I did not find it easy. Still we were fortunate, No. 52 escaped any damage, time passed and the day of my readmission to work in Kent arrived: October 24th, 1940.

And so we were back in the same bungalow and settled down to the former routine as if it had never been interrupted. Work was plentiful but I enjoyed it, and though a very few people deliberately kept out of my way because of my origin as a supposed enemy alien, on the whole people appeared to take to me. Mrs Porterfield was not only my steady helper but also my eyes and ears, telling me whenever I made a faux pas according to local customs. I had not realised that patients expected a medicine with every consultation even if there was no need for it, and after I had been warned of that I always made a point of explaining why I had not given a medicine if I had failed to do so. There were also some simple household remedies I preferred to order in suitable cases rather than strictly medical treatment, and later on — when I had completely settled in and forged affectionate bonds with most of my patients — I was told by more than one that the local populace had agreed they would, on my death, have inscribed on my head-stone, "Gargle with tea" on one side and, "Inhale with bicarbonate of soda" on the other!

My readmission to this area for work meant that I was exempt from curfew, permitted to use a motor car, and free to go to any place in the area forbidden even to local people who were not actually resident in that area. I am thinking particularly of a specially guarded and fortified small peninsula containing the sewage works and houses of employees, many of whom with their families were patients of mine. My wife was still subject to curfew, as at that time the only reason for exemption was fire-watching, and she was unable to volunteer for that duty having to be ready to answer the telephone at home.

One remaining restriction was that I had to report whenever I left and returned to our specially protected area, almost entirely for trips to London to meet our daughter from the school train or take her back to Paddington Station; there, one of the nuns from the convent met all the pupils and took them back to Devon. Whenever possible, of course, we combined these outings to London with a visit to the Colles or the Fletchers and therefore tried to leave early in the morning. This presented difficulties, as the Aliens Officer to whom we had to report did not come on duty until 9 a.m. However, I evidently got on with the police very well even then, because when I explained my predicament the inspector said: "Alright, just report on your return, after all when you are out of the district you cannot get into mischief here."

The Police Force in Rainham then consisted of Sergeant O'Keefe and two regular constables, augmented in the evening by some "specials" led by Sergeant Knowles. He was of particular help to me. One evening he came and said: "Doctor you forgot to put the lights on your car so I have done it for you." Another time he told me he had a complaint from a local resident about my black-out not being efficient and offered to come next morning to check it and put it right.

The only other restriction was that the possession of a wireless was forbidden. Aliens were allowed to listen but not to handle a wireless set themselves; the reason being, so I understood, that one could send out even from a receiving set Morse signals which could be picked up by enemy aircraft. However, it was not very long before Sergeant Knowles told me that I could now apply for exemption from this restriction. He and his family had meanwhile become patients of mine and he had actually bought a set for me from a man who was about to leave the country and Knowles was going to hand it to me as soon as permission had arrived. A few weeks passed and one of Churchill's famous broadcasts was announced which I was very anxious to hear. "I shall put the wiring in so that we only have to connect the set if permission arrives at the last moment," Knowles assured me.

111

My first car in front of our house.

The evening came and the permit had still not arrived, but half an hour before the broadcast there was a knock on the door. Sergeant O'Keefe and Sergeant Knowles, both in uniform, Knowles with a wireless set in his arms, stood there. "We too would like to hear Churchill so we thought we would bring the set, listen together and then take it away again," they told me and this we did. Soon afterwards the permit arrived.

The air raids in our area increased, and more and more people, whose presence in the district was not essential, were anxious to leave. I was told that Dr Porterfield owned a second house in South Avenue, Gillingham, which had been built by a partner of his who had left, and then for a time was let privately. His tenants now asked if they could be released from their contract. Would I like to rent the house for £1 a week? The prospect was marvellous. A home of our own again, and a saving of money, because the storage of our Viennese furniture, which had arrived at the London Docks in the last ship before the outbreak of war, was costing more than that rent. A week before Christmas we moved into the house, which I much later bought, and where we continued living for 37 years. Three days after leaving the bungalow in Pump Lane three incendiary bombs came through the roof, two landing in the armchairs where we used to sit in the evening.

Having been built as a doctor's house, 25 South Avenue contained a purpose-built surgery and I at once decided to open a branch surgery there. I had enough furniture and equipment for the consulting room, but I needed chairs for the waiting room. When I asked Dr Porterfield he said: "Oh, I have got one for you." "One?" I said, rather surprised. He thought one would do for a beginning but actually produced three. I was later told that the South Avenue surgery had always been considered a white elephant, and both the Porterfields were rather surprised and gratified when soon an extra six chairs had to be bought.

Not long afterwards Dr Porterfield was posted away and he then suggested work with the two surgeries might become too much for me, now that he could no longer lend a helping hand. However, I was determined to keep on with it. After all, I reasoned, I had to enlarge the practice if it was to maintain two partners after the war, and we came to an arrangement that I would be paid a percentage on every new patient I got in the branch surgery, though of course not on those who simply transferred from the Rainham surgery because they lived closer to South Avenue.

During the Christmas vacation our daughter Gabriele developed measles and my wife contracted it from her. Gabriele got over it easily but my wife, in an early pregnancy at the time, developed pneumonia, miscarried, and was quite ill. However, nobody wanted to go into hospital with the air raids on if they could possibly help it, and so she was kept at home. The Queen's nurse (fore-runner of the district nurse) was very helpful indeed.

That winter was one of the hardest in living memory, and snow was about as bad as in the later winter of 1947. This made visits to the outlying villages some-what difficult, especially at night, and one in particular remains in my memory when, on the way to Upchurch in an air raid, one tyre got a puncture and I had to change the wheel in the road which ran between fields. But I always felt that I was still better off than the fighting men.

Even so, there was one occasion on which I felt at the end of my tether. I had just come back from a round of many visits when Mrs Porterfield told me she had three more. "Tell them the doctor has just died," was my reaction. It was the only time I remember being irritable with Ngaire and really felt I could not go on. But I did, and it is still a source of pride to me that never before, during or after my work in the National Health Service, have I refused a call.

The war went on, work went on, but so did home life. Soon after my wife had recovered from her miscarriage she was expecting a baby again, and in February 1942, our son Francis was born. He was a tubby, very placid baby, and it probably helped a lot that we kept him very quiet even during the noisy air raid nights. There was a shelter at the bottom of our garden, but we never went there, as I always held that it was better to have the doubtful risk of a bomb to the almost certain risk of pneumonia! However, when the Morrison table shelters were introduced my wife with Francis slept in it, our daughter Gabriele, of course, being only at home during school holidays.

It was early in that winter of 1942 my car got stuck in the snow in Stockbury, one of the small outlying villages, and the back axle broke. I had meanwhile made friends with Dick Cushing who had a garage in Rainham and looked after my car, and it was then that I appreciated what a real friend meant. No spare parts were available, but Cushing got on the telephone and located a suitable secondhand back axle at a car breaker's in Dover. He drove there in melting snow, fog and shelling from the French coast, brought the axle home, and after thirty-six hours I was on the road again. During those thirty-six hours I tried to do on a bicycle whatever visits I could, but not having ridden one for some twenty-five years I was not very good at it and found it very exhausting. Incidentally, I discovered that my permit to use a motor car did not include a bicycle and I hastened to apply for this separate exemption. By the time it arrived, I used a bicycle very rarely, but nobody seemed to mind that I had anticipated the official permit.

When talking to old Father Mellitus of Buckfast, I had told him that, spiritually, we felt very isolated in our parish. The Irish parish priest was a violent anti-communist to the extent that he thought and hoped God would use Hitler to defeat communism, and then deal with Hitler in His own way. I suggested to him that the German danger was much nearer to us and I preferred people who said "There is no God" to Hitler who virtually said "God, that's me". Though anti-communist myself, I felt that it would be very much better if we defeated the Nazis and hoped that God would later deal with the communists in His own way. Later on, when Father Scott was older and had mellowed and become a patient of mine, he accepted my ideas, we became friends, and remained so until he retired to a monastery in Ireland, and even then kept up a correspondence until he died.

Still, in those early days as I explained to Father Mellitus, things were somewhat difficult for my wife and myself. "Our abbot sometimes comes your way visiting Ramsgate Abbey," he said, "I shall tell him to look in on you. He is a very good abbot, he does as he is told — I was his novice master," he said with a twinkle in his eye. He was as good as his word. Abbot Bruno stopped on his way to visit us, and when leaving asked me for advice regarding one of his knees. The abbey doctor had said it was arthritis, but treatment did not help. I looked at it, thought the trouble was due to a varicose vein behind the knee, and wrote to the abbey doctor, apologising that I had seen the abbot whilst he was on a friendly visit to us and, therefore, could not get his permission in advance. I told him my diagnosis.

Dr Williams, elderly, not a Catholic himself, but a great friend of the abbey, asked Father Abbot to write to me. He had said: "I think the man is right, I don't know why I didn't think of it myself. Anyway, I don't do the treatment myself and will have to send you somewhere; will you write and ask if he would undertake the treatment." This the abbot did, and asked how long it would take and if there was anywhere near us he could stay. I replied that I would be delighted to inject his vein, we had a guest room though very shabbily furnished (which it was!) and as I wanted to see the result, treatment would take eight days. Would

114

he come and stay with us? This was the first of many stays of Abbot Bruno in our house; the treatment was a success and he invited me then that whenever I came that way I should stay at the abbey as his guest, and not at the guest house. Recovering from a short, sharp attack of tonsillitis I first made use of his invitation in November 1942, and have since stayed there on many occasions, even after his resignation because of failing eye-sight. After the death of Abbot Bruno his successor, Abbot Placid, wrote to me saying he hoped I would still come and stay whenever the opportunity arose.

Meanwhile I was also in contact with two other abbeys. To Downside I had first been before the war, when Father Leander looked after me in a sort of private retreat, and we remained in correspondence until his death; my son was later to go to school there. The other abbey I visited several times was Prinknash in Gloucestershire, where my mother's youngest brother had found shelter and hospitality when he — also a refugee — came to this country sponsored again by the Colles, who had been friends of Dyer Edwards who gave the Prinknash Estate to the monks. He had much changed since the days of his gay bachelorhood, had become a practising Catholic and a Franciscan tertiary, taking his faith and the Order's regulations very seriously indeed. As an artist he helped in the pottery, which was then in its infancy but is now one of the famous potteries in the country, and it was through visiting him that I made friends there. Abbot Upson later became a great friend of ours who visited us several times, and said Mass in the house which was then a special privilege, traditional only to Benedictine abbots. Each of the abbeys had its peculiar character, each a fascination of its own, but nowhere did I feel as much at home as in Buckfast.

The war continued and life and work did not change very much though the war news became a little more promising with the menace of the U-boats being overcome. Still our area remained closely guarded, and anybody wanting to come into it from outside had to show a good reason for it. This led to the rather comical situation that one day, when Harry and Hester were to visit us to see our home and discuss several practicalities, I had to stand guarantee for them who were my guarantors when coming to this country. They took it in good part and I do not think I have ever seen them laugh so much. "You certainly have arrived," was their comment.

Some time previously I had offered to Dr Hoby — who was then in charge of the Home Guard and happened also to be our family doctor — that I would be very willing to volunteer for work in the Home Guard if he could make any use of me; I emphasised at the same time that I would not be offended if it was thought best if I kept my nose out of it. "I know you well enough to recommend you when a vacancy occurs," was his reply, and it was not all that long before a vacancy did occur. It was at Lodge Hill, some eight miles from home, and meant a drive through the artificial smoke screen which every evening was thrown across the river. "Would I be prepared to accept it?" I said: "Yes, of course, provided I am given the necessary petrol." It was a horrible journey with masked headlamps, driving to and fro through what was practically a dense fog, to act as

102 Rocket Battery at Beaty Avenue, Gillingham.

As a Major in the Home Guard during the war.

medical officer to the Home Guard section of a mixed battery manned by Royal Artillery and Home Guard. The men, of course, went to the site in the evening and home next morning, but I had to look after Dr Porterfield's practice as well and therefore had to go to the site late in the evening and come home in the night, being all the time on call for emergencies both for the practice and for the Home Guard.

As an alien of enemy origin, my appointment had to be confirmed by the War Office, while the routine appointments of Home Guard officers were issued by the ack-ack command. Would I be prepared to act for the time being in civilian clothes, issued with a special pass? Of course I again agreed. It was the time when service in the Home Guard had become compulsory for British men, and many would have preferred to take a well paid overtime job in the evening. Hence there were plenty of applications for release with which I had to deal. "What have you done hitherto?" was my question to everybody who claimed he was not fit to continue in the Home Guard. "Light duties sir." "And what is light duty?" "Guard and first-aid." "What first-aid training have you had?" "None sir," was the inevitable reply.

I could not let this continue. I was only too well aware that if anything happened at the gun site and the first-aid teams were inefficient, the question would be asked: "Who is the medical officer?" and I would be in danger of being blamed for sabotaging the war effort. Few men succeeded in their claim for release, but immediately I set up a concentrated programme of first-aid training. It meant going to the gun site practically every evening and I usually had a meal with the officers in their mess. But I felt satisfied that the organisation improved

Standing in front of my second car in Major's uniform.

and with it the morale of the men, who now felt that they had a worthwhile task. I also managed to get stores of first-aid equipment together.

Apart from first-aid training, I fulfilled the usual tasks of a medical officer, looking after the health and treating any injuries to the men. Though officially responsible only for the Home Guard contingent, in fact the regulars of the Royal Artillery also usually came to me. They had a part-time medical officer of their own, but this was a lady doctor, and in those days this was not accepted as readily as it is now, and therefore most men consulted a male medical officer whenever possible.

Routine continued, but as time passed I got somewhat disappointed with my commission being so long delayed. I pressed the adjutant, who had me issued with a uniform so that everything should be ready once the appointment arrived from the Home Office. Italy had by now capitulated, the Sharnhorst had been sunk off the North Cape and the allied troops had landed at Anzio. One had the first inkling that war might soon come to an end, and with it the urgency of my official appointment increased for me. I felt that I had proved myself and it was about time that this should be officially recognised. I also knew that a commission would be helpful in enabling me to get priority for naturalisation, once one could apply for it. I decided to take the bull by the horns and told the adjutant that at my next attendance I would come in uniform "pips or no pips". Evidently he thought I was joking, and just made comforting noises that the commission should arrive at any moment. "There won't be any pips," he added, "there will be a crown." I did not believe that I would be appointed major as most of my British colleagues who were medical officers in the Home Guard were captains, and I learned only later that the rank went with the appointment and mine, covering the main guns defending the dockyard, was graded as so important that it carried appointment as a major.

As there was no emergency I let two days elapse, and then drove up to the gun site in uniform, of course without any badge of rank. I met the adjutant on the way to the camp and offered him a lift. He looked at me and said: "Heavens man I shall be shot." "Why?" I enquired, looking innocent. "You are not properly dressed." "How is that? I am in the Home Guard am I not?" "Yes," he said reluctantly. "But I have no rank have I?" "No," he said, even more reluctantly. "Well then, I can wear uniform but without any badge of rank. Of course, I can go to the men's mess if you prefer." "You can't do that," he said despairingly.

I had my evening meal in the officers' mess, being treated as if a crown were floating invisibly above my shoulders! There was only one other major on the site, the commanding officer of the battery, a Major Venner. I took him aside after supper and told him the same tale I had told Captain Fuller, the adjutant. "My dear chap," he said, "I don't mind if you come in uniform, in civies, or in bathing suit so long as you come. Anyway, I shall again urge your appointment." Whether or not it was the result of my action I would not know, but three days later my commission arrived. With it I was exempted from the last restrictions and Magda, now the wife of a British commissioned officer, was no longer subject to curfew. Captain Fuller was not shot because of me, but very unfortunately shot himself a little later and I was called to the armoury where he had been found dead. Everybody was very shocked by his death as he was a most pleasant and well liked man. I had never acted as his doctor, but was later told that he had been suffering from high blood pressure.

It was the time of the V1 flying bombs, of which more fell on Kent than on London. Many of them were shot down into the sea from the coast, but almost all happened in the south and west of Kent. In spite of heavy casualties and much material damage, one sensed that the war was coming to a victorious end before very long. North Kent, where I lived and where the battery was situated, escaped very lightly. I actually had the impression that Major Venner felt somewhat frustrated by this when he gave his usual toast at the evening meal: "Happy days and noisy nights." He would have liked his guns to go into action much more often.

Chapter 12
THE PARTNERSHIP

During that time Dr Porterfield came home more often. After his ship had been torpedoed at sea, but he had escaped unharmed, he was given a shore appointment before ultimately being posted to India. On one such occasion he asked me for my future plans; did I still want a partnership? If so, we should make arrangements soon because, when the war ended, all the doctors coming home from the war would want to settle in practice, and my position as an alien would possibly be a handicap in the competition. Of course I wanted a partnership, but I was aware that, at that time with the war still on, no bank or insurance company would lend me the money. Dr Porterfield asked me to come round one evening to discuss matters with him and his wife. I do not think that any partnership was ever agreed more easily and informally. The purchase price of a two-fifths share in the practice was very fair, and instead of borrowing money and paying it back to a bank or insurance company I should just pay the purchase price in instalments to him. "What is the interest rate to be?" I asked. "Interest, that is too difficult mathematics, let's forget about interest," was Dr Porterfield's reply, and I shall always be grateful to him and Ngaire for thus having made the partnership possible for me.

The next thing was to apply for permission to the Home Office and on January 11th 1945 I was informed that "the Secretary of State does not desire to raise any objection to Dr Pollaczek entering into partnership with Dr Porterfield in Rainham as proposed". Now the Deed could be drawn up and the partnership started on April 5th 1945, the date being chosen to coincide with the financial year, which made book-keeping easier.

By that time Dr Porterfield had been posted abroad, but he sent me for the day a letter of good wishes for myself and the practice. Mrs Porterfield decided that, even in his absence, there should be a formal celebration and invited his two best doctor friends, Chalmers and Campbell. The men wore dinner jackets, she and my wife evening dress. It was a real dinner party, a rare treat during the war years. Time passed quickly and the party was just about to break up near midnight when the telephone rang. It was one of our midwives who wanted me for a confinement, and the next hours were taken up with the delivery of a 12 lb. baby, the biggest I can remember in my practice. The surroundings were not ideal for the forceps delivery which was necessary. The place was a small, old cottage in one of the surrounding villages, the only light came from a portable paraffin lamp, and my evening wear — in those days one still wore a stiff-breasted shirt with dinner jacket — must have provided a strange contrast. However, all went well, and as the family doctor I later saw the baby growing up into a healthy youngster.

First Aid Class for the Home Guard after the war (with the instructor Charlie Graham).

Soon afterwards, on May 9th, the European war came to an end and just over three months later the Japanese war as well. Four days later, on August 18th, our younger daughter, Veronica, was born. A joyous event to celebrate victory and a token of our confidence in the future.

Doctors never treat members of their own family, but as it happened Dr Hoby, our family doctor, came a bit late and I felt I had to "scrub up" in readiness for any emergency. I was just ready and so was the baby when Dr Hoby arrived. "No time left for me to prepare," he said, "I shall watch you as you bring your child into the world." It is strange how even as a father one suddenly becomes all doctor. Everything went smoothly according to the book, and Dr Hoby and the midwife were just spectators.

Demobilisation was now progressing. Soon Dr Porterfield came home and we reorganised the practice. He took over his end based on the Rainham surgery; I continued mainly the Gillingham side, based on the former branch surgery in South Avenue. Of course some patients who had never had Dr Porterfield even though they were registered in his name when I was assistant, stayed with me, but I remember particularly one of his old patients, the eldest of several sisters, who had originally been full of moans when I took over the practice of Dr Porterfield. She now decided to stay with me. "You can't do that," I said, "you

121

My brother Hery in the Argentine in 1946.   Magda with Francis 1944.

are one of his very old patients and he will immediately enquire after you, and probably come and visit you." "That will be a social visit," she insisted, "I know what I shall tell him: one can get used to anything so I got used to you."

Unlike today's partnerships we both attended to our patients individually, taking off only one half day each including the night and alternate weekends from Saturday lunchtime to Monday morning.

The four of us quickly became firm friends, and when my mother joined my wife and me in England in November 1945, she too was accepted by the Porterfields as one of the family.

Mother and I had been in written contact all during the war but it was rather sporadic, and we never felt really at ease because of the possiblity of German censorship. I actually have in my possession a postcard which — though posted in Geneva and addressed to me here — bears the stamp, complete with swastika, as having been passed by the German military authorities.

Mother had had a hard time during the war. Having originally left Vienna without any difficulty with her Czech passport, she had lived for a time in Prague, very modestly but without real financial worries. However, whilst she was on holiday with friends in Switzerland, the Nazi occupation of Czechoslovakia happened and cut off her return. For a while she stayed on with those friends, but in time it seems the relationship became somewhat strained, and with the help of several people, prominent among them my father's youngest sister Hedwig, then living in Israel, she went to a small, comparatively cheap, pension. Even this, however, could not be long term, and eventually she was accepted, almost penniless, into a Salvation Army hostel in Geneva. It was during this time of hardship that she, who had been the strongest critic of our becoming Catholics, became herself converted and was received into the Catholic church by the Dominican Père de Menasce. This and the hope of reunion with us carried her over every hardship.

Of course I myself felt happy that we would see her again, but, at the same time, I must admit to some apprehension and this for two reasons both of which I felt would lead to her disappointment. One was the emotionalism of her which I felt I could not match being of a much more even temperament. The other was that she evidently had visions of all hardships being now over and she would have here a comfortable life. She never realised how hard up we were ourselves. Of course her expectations were small compared with what she was used to in her previous life — even if to a steadily diminishing degree — up to her involvement in the war. A small two-roomed flat with a part-time daily help near us was all she expected! And when I tried to explain to her that all we could offer was our rather primitive guest room, sharing the remainder of the house with us, her only reaction was that she evidently would soon have to find other accommodation. How she imagined this would happen I have never understood. We decided it would be best if my wife stayed at home to prepare the welcome for my mother, while Ngaire Porterfield came with me to the airport in case my mother needed some female assistance, as she actually did. Luckily my mother took to Ngaire immediately and so everything went as I had hoped, the English language which, of course, we had to use (Ngaire not speaking German) taking the dramatics out of the situation. By the time we arrived home and settled to long, quiet talks it was a normal happy atmosphere.

Unfortunately, as I had feared, mother's happiness did not last very long. I was busy with the practice, Magda busy with our youngest child then about 3½ months old, and our son then not quite 4, tired mother, though in the morning he was for a few hours in play school. She also missed having any of her old friends around, or anybody with literary leanings or understanding of her own literary works. London, where she still had some acquaintances and where she hoped for literary connections, was out of reach for her from us and it soon became clear that if she was to settle down in this country it could only be in London. With the help of friends we found her accommodation in a convent situated near Swiss Cottage, where she had a bed-sitting room at a cost which my Aunt Hedwig and I between us could afford. My mother had also expected, and in several letters from Geneva had pressed for, help from my brother but this was never forthcoming. He himself lived under very primitive circumstances on a dairy farm in the Argentine. Though he was at that time manager of a farm which secured his living, his only hope of actual cash was from the sales of a small herd and produce which he was allowed to keep for himself. However, he remained always the same, and though he said he would send money if and when he could, he had always spent it before he had actually earned it and so never had anything over to send! He suggested that he could keep mother on the farm if she was willing to go to the Argentine, but told me that she had refused, finding the

Our 3 children in 1947.

living conditions he could offer her too primitive, and I feel sure that she would have been worse off with him than with us.

However, again London was a disappointment and though we did our best to visit her as often as possible she became more and more lonely and longed to return to Vienna.

Her younger sister had died during the war in a concentration camp. In spite of having been a Catholic for many years, she was taken from a convent where she was teaching languages. Of her three children, the girl and her husband died in a concentration camp, and the two boys were never heard of again. Mother's youngest brother, who had lived in Prinknash Abbey, had died some months before her arrival and was buried in the cemetery there. However, mother still had in Vienna the elder of her two brothers, who had been fortunate having a privileged position among the Jewish population because, while an officer in the first world war, he had received an unusually high decoration for bravery. This service to the "Fatherland" was acknowledged by the Nazis in-so-far as he was allowed to carry on life at home with his Aryan wife, and though he was no longer allowed to continue his practice as a lawyer he could eke out a living by practising as some sort of legal adviser. His wife stood loyally by him all the time and they managed to send their son to the United States. It must have been a hard wrench for them, aggravated for my uncle by the fact that it meant for him also parting from his beloved violin. This, being an old Pietro Guaneri — more or less equal to a Stradivarius I am told — was the only possession of value the boy could take with him inconspicuously, and it evidently gave him a start in the new life. He became a civil engineer.

During the time my mother was in England Uncle Otto had resumed his lawyer's practice, his wife died, and he then went on a visit to his son in the United States. However, after his return, he was able and willing to arrange for mother to travel back to Vienna and to maintain her there in more congenial surroundings, with some contributions from Aunt Hedwig and myself. However, this was not until towards the end of 1948.

Meantime, the practice went on smoothly and for my part very happily, and when Dr Porterfield said he wanted to go for a few weeks to New Zealand to see his family I was quite ready to carry on, though as the practice had grown a lot, a locum was needed for part of the time.

It was, therefore, a great shock to me when I received a letter from Norman telling me that he wanted a divorce and that he and Ngaire had spoken about it several times. Ngaire had always very loyally kept it from me that there were any difficulties in the marriage, so I was unprepared. However, I had to face facts. Norman made it quite clear that he was not going to return from New Zealand if he would not be given his freedom. He said that he was enjoying the practice and work with me, found the partnership pleasant and felt the future would hold good prospects and happy times, but he was unable to give his best under the present circumstances. If Ngaire did not consent he intended to stay in New Zealand to open a practice there, giving the Rainham practice to me.

It was the time when the National Health Service was on the horizon and it was quite uncertain if, and what, compensation one would get; to sell Norman's share in the practice during the period of uncertainty was out of the question. I certainly did not want to make capital out of the difficulties of Norman and Ngaire, and I wrote to Norman in those terms. Of course I could not deal alone with this question, but consulted with Bert Trott, the Porterfield's best friend. Between us we arranged with Ngaire that she would go and see her family in New Zealand, leaving a few days before Norman's return, which I considered most urgent as decisions about the National Health Service had to be made very soon. Meanwhile, Ngaire — who held an authority from her husband — gave me notice on his behalf that he was intending to withdraw from the partnership, as such a declaration was legally required, but we agreed that this would be kept open for him to revoke after his return. I still hoped that the whole affair would settle down after a time of separation, but alas things did not turn out that way and divorce proceedings followed, Ngaire moved out of the district and Norman remarried. Their son John remained in boarding school and shared his holidays between his father and mother.

The partnership carried on and Norman and I still remained friendly, but it was no longer quite the same. Moreover, when the National Health Service was introduced, a maximum number of 4,000 patients was allowed per doctor, and 8,000 for a partnership of two, but a doctor could keep any over this number

Abbot Bruno of Buckfast in our garden.

who were on his list at the time though he could not take on any more. On our joint list we had well over this number, slightly over 5,000 in the name of Dr Porterfield and about 3,200 in my name. Consequently we decided to dissolve our partnership. It meant that Dr Porterfield could keep all his patients, though his list was closed for new ones, and I could build up my list in which Dr Porterfield helped by sending on to me patients who applied to him for acceptance. Our mutual relief arrangements remained the same as during our partnership, and we agreed that I would buy the house which I had rented from him and, as a sitting tenant, he let me have it at an advantageous price. The actual dissolution of the partnership took place in April 1949, at the end of the financial year following the introduction of the National Health Service.

Chapter 13
MY OWN N.H.S. PRACTICE

I had now my own practice and our own house, and with it the foundation of a happy future, but though I and those around me had escaped any direct suffering from the war (apart from that to which every individual was exposed), I was the poorer for the loss of a great friend and benefactor, Harry Colles, who died suddenly a few months before its end. Of course we kept in close contact with Hester all the time until she herself suddenly died in 1952. Of my own family there were now left only one brother of my mother's in Vienna, she herself had died there in 1950, and my own brother living in the Argentine.

I remained in the National Health Service until the end of 1967, and then continued another ten years in private practice. Having thus had experience before the introduction of the National Health Service, in the National Health Service and — after resigning from it — again in private practice, I would say that there was no essential difference between these three periods of my medical work though the number of patients at the time of the National Health Service was, of course, larger. It was large indeed because, at the time, the maximum number was 4,000 patients, and though this was later reduced to 3,500, each doctor was allowed to keep the patients he had at the time of the reduction, though he was not allowed to take on more except members of the same family. Thus, as by then I had a little over 3,900 patients, my list was closed.

Thinking back to those days when Dr Porterfield and I had — and tried to keep — the maximum number of patients allowed, it seems strange that it is now considered desirable to lower the number on a doctor's list even below the present average. I saw recently in a medical paper the figure of 1,700 to 1,900 quoted as optimum to give doctors the necessary time to deal adequately with their patients. It is true that in the bad season of the year we doctors had little time to ourselves, but I am sure the patients never went short of attention; as a matter of fact I always thought that the most essential thing for a doctor was to have time for his patients.

We had no appointments system and I am still not convinced of its advantages. From what I observe, it seems that patients now have to wait for days to get an appointment rather than taking their turn in the surgery, when they were certain to be seen the same day, even if it meant a wait of several hours which nobody seemed to mind. I was probably the only doctor who had no morning but an afternoon surgery from 2 o'clock onwards and many patients from the outlying villages brought their sandwiches. Of course there was also an evening surgery meant for those returning from work, which then was much later than now.

This idea of an afternoon surgery was one I perpetuated from my time on the continent where it was the usual thing. It left me free to do all the urgent home visits in the morning, and after all it is the bed-ridden ones who want to see their doctor as soon as possible. The early afternoon, after the cooking is done, is usually a fairly quiet time for housewives, a time when the weather is best for small children and elderly people, and if they came early enough (and we opened the door of the waiting room one-and-a-half hours in advance) mothers could manage to get away in time to collect their older children from school. From what I was told this idea worked well with my patients, who treated the surgery as the occasion of an animated party, exchanging all the latest gossip.

There was then, as there is now, a lot of talk about the abuse of the National Health Service, but I never seemed to encounter it to any unreasonable degree. Of course there were unnecessary calls, but nearly always I could understand why the patient or the relative got worried, and thought that the call *was* necessary, and in some other cases the simple-mindedness of the people gave a ready explanation for the call. I never forgot the words of my senior surgeon in Vienna, who coined a new phrase from the Latin word pecus (cattle). He called it "pecuditas" which probably would be best translated into "cattle-mindedness", and he always impressed on the juniors that pecuditas is no safeguard against illness. Thus I always went cheerfully to those people wondering what I would find. In the very few cases in which the call was obviously frivolous I explained to the family, after my examination of the patient, that I did not think they were right in calling me but as they had done so in order to give as quick relief as possible they would now have to go to the chemist at once. Very often the chemist was far, but I volunteered to take them there "though to my regret I could not take them back". Particularly if it was raining, in the night when no buses were running – and few people then had a car – this proved to be a very healthy lesson! and after we had parted on the best of terms I never had a second frivolous call from the same family. If the call proved to be necessary I nearly always managed to find a suitable first-aid treatment in my bag to tide them over until the morning.

Some people seem to think that the abuse of the Health Service has increased over the years, but in the beginning we thought the opposite was true. It seemed that, with the new possibility of calling the doctor without fear of the cost, many believed that he was now at the beck and call of everybody, but gradually it was possible to educate one's patients to the best possible use of the service with benefit to both parties, and hardly ever did this cause bad feeling. As far as I can remember during the twenty years of my National Health Service practice I took four families off my list, and the only trouble I had was with one man who threatened to appeal to the Member of Parliament for the district complaining that I did not want to treat him any longer. Obviously he was not very lucky in this, and it may be significant that much later, when he had died, I was again in touch and very friendly with his family, though I never had them back as patients.

Of course in the early days with most patients having then no conveyance, the doctor had to do many calls in cases where, later, patients were able to come to the surgery in their own or their neighbour's car. But to see a patient in his home surroundings leads to much closer contact with the whole family, and I am convinced that the modern tendency of seeing people mainly in the surgery has contributed a lot to the loosening of personal relationships. All this depends to a large extent on the view one takes of the doctor's task. To me it has always meant to be the friend, philosopher and medical adviser. For any Christian doctor who takes his beliefs seriously this might be a demanding, but extremely satisfying role.

Of all the cases in my practice, the one that I remember with the greatest pleasure — and almost pride — was of a woman who came to see me complaining that her teenage daughter had recently brought home very bad school reports. "I can't talk to Susie, perhaps you can doctor," she said, and I very willingly and successfully undertook this task. I am sure I helped the family much more with this than I would have done by medical treatment at several routine medical attendances.

Of course there were plenty of serious cases as well in the daily routine but that routine differed in many ways from the present. Infections of any kind, now that many antibiotics are freely available, are no longer serious illnesses, and many patients who then needed daily visiting now require only one visit. Other patients who were incurable then are still incurable, but while the doctor in earlier days made frequent visits to them, he now has practice-nurses and symptom control teams to take some of the burden from him. The change came so gradually that it is not possible to pinpoint the time at which it occurred.

I myself feel that technical progress had reduced the human element in the doctor's work, but I suppose this is a consequence, following as a matter of course upon the altered lifestyle of people, which itself was the result of altered conditions and surroundings. That again was a gradual process which is still continuing.

When we moved to South Avenue, which fronts the main London-Dover Road, but is divided from it by some lawn and a hedge, there were behind us, houses for only a short distance, and then the open country started with meadows and fields full of wild flowers, among which I particularly remember the poppies with their bright red colour. Now a council estate has replaced them, but fortunately it is still only a short drive in the car until one finds oneself in the "garden of England" with its fruit farms, hop fields and, in season, newly born lambs.

But the change is still continuing as it has done for many years. Even our house, which I am told was the first to be built in South Avenue, dates back no further than 1934; before then our road was the tramline from Chatham to Rainham. When I started practice here, Rainham was still very much a village on its own — now Gillingham and Rainham have both grown, so that they are now fully joined and development is still progressing on the other side of Rainham. This growth is underlined by the new Gillingham Police Station having been built in Rainham, which is gradually spreading into the countryside towards the villages of Upchurch to the east and Bredhurst to the south. However, the old

Jean Flavin (then my secretary) and I.

centres of Rainham, as well as those of Bredhurst, Upchurch and other villages still retain much of their original character, as do the older people, even those whose houses were replaced by more modern ones. Some of the old features have now disappeared. I still remember most elderly ladies opening the door wearing a hat! I have never found out whether they wore a hat all day or put it on when they heard a knock on the door — and I was too shy to ask — but it is now a very long time since I last observed that custom. The essentials of village spirit — politeness and good-neighbourliness — are still very much alive.

Whilst, therefore, not much can be said about the medical part of general practice without going into clinical details, for which this is certainly not the place, something must be said about the family doctor's midwifery practice which, in those days, was almost entirely domiciliary and very demanding.

Originally we had only two midwives to cover Rainham, though the outlying villages had usually a nurse/midwife of their own. All the midwives were strong personalities, and the two in Rainham, with whom I shared most of my cases, were very different characters and each had her distinctive group of fans. One, Nurse Maisey, I would say about forty years old, had previously been a theatre sister, and always retained the distinctive trait: efficient, neat and somewhat autocratic, she would give her orders to the patients, albeit to their benefit. The other, Midwife Greenwood, was much older, the last of those who was a midwife without ever having been a State Registered Nurse. Efficient, but easy-going and kindly, though not always delicate. I always remember coming to a patient's house where she was already in attendance upstairs, when I heard a loud slap —

130

evidently applied to the bare bottom of the woman in labour — accompanied by the shout: "Don't claw me, you cat." When I got upstairs the atmosphere was again quite harmonious, and both seemed to have forgotten the little incident.

The doctor was called as a matter of course to every confinement, and only if serious complications arose was the patient sent to hospital. Normally, every forceps delivery was done at home, and there was only one such delivery in which I failed during all the years of my practice; the confinement was then safely completed by Caesarean section in hospital and all was well. Also, breech deliveries I did myself, at first all of them, but in later years I had to send first confinements with breech presentation to hospital because I realised that if anything should go wrong no consultant would back me. Before then, however, I remember the breech delivery of a 42 year old primipara, whose then baby girl twenty years later herself became a mother, and was delivered by me at home.

Another incident still very alive in my mind is that of two young women, booked with the same midwife, starting labour at the same time. We arranged that the midwife would sit with one, I with the other, and that every hour we would change over, meeting each other on the way to exchange latest news. If one of us did not show up at the rendezvous it meant that the birth was on the way. The plan worked like clock-work, and later in the day, within one hour, we had first a forceps and then a breech delivery. I suppose by today's standard the arrangements were horrifying, but they worked. The "do-it-yourself" practice was extremely satisfying, I never lost a mother nor a baby during confinement though I had a very few still-births of babies who had died in the last stages of pregnancy. In the care of their personal doctor, their personal midwife and their own family, all the young mothers were very happy. It was only in later years that husbands were encouraged to be present at the birth, but ever since I experienced an expectant father fainting and falling to the floor when he watched an episiotomy, my encouragment was somewhat muted and I always asked: "Are you sure you won't faint? I shall have no time to attend to you." I had no trouble since, and actually most of the modern fathers seem to be made of sterner stuff and indeed can be quite helpful.

Certainly maternity work was a very uniting factor between doctor and patient, and so was another of my "specialities", that of doing all my own minor surgery. Though this was not paid under the National Health Service rules, I loved doing it and I never minded the small expense to myself. After all, it was not more than the price of a theatre or even only a cinema ticket, and gave me at least as much pleasure. I reaped the benefit later on because, when I was in private practice, a great number of my former patients stuck to me, recommended others and, with the consent of their own doctor, I even operated on numerous people who were not my regular private patients but came to me just to have a toe-nail, a cyst or some other "lump" removed, to have their baby sons circumcised or even an umbilical rupture operated on.

The intimate relationship with the patients and their families made it also very easy to be truthful to them in cases of serious illness. Of course I was

131

occasionally asked by the wife of a patient suffering from cancer: "Harry doesn't know what he is suffering from, you won't tell him doctor will you?" My answer was always the same: "I shall not lie if I am asked a direct question, but I never volunteer answers to questions which are not asked." My patients were quite aware of my attitude, and those who did not want to hear the truth never asked me a direct question.

A good illustration is the case of a woman with inoperable lung cancer who developed pneumonia which had to be treated in spite of the underlying incurable illness to relieve the distressing shortness of breath. "Doctor, shall I get well again?" the patient asked. "You are very seriously ill just now, I would not know, but there is always hope. Ask me again in three days and I shall answer your question." After three days the woman felt much better and never asked me the question again. On the other hand, I can recall patients to whom I gave the diagnosis of cancer in answer to a direct question, who said: "I am glad you have told me Doctor — had you said otherwise I would not have believed you." Prior to receiving such confirmation, the harmony of many families was upset by husband, wife and children evading the whole issue; once the knowledge was shared, they could discuss the situation and often felt much more at peace.

Whatever the diagnosis, however, I never took away hope, nor did I give, even to the relations, an estimate of how much time a patient might have left to live. The mistakes that have been made are numerous, and, thinking back to my own experience during an illness as a young hospital surgeon, prevented me from making the same error.

On the other hand I was probably something of a tyrant to any patient where I felt it essential to force compliance. Thus I often returned to a house earlier than I had said and remember one such occasion when, on knocking at the front door, I heard hurried barefoot steps inside. Suspicious of the patient whom I had, with good reason, confined to bed, I pushed open the flap of the letter-box just in time to see a pair of naked legs disappear up the stairs. To the patient's lame excuse that she had not expected me to revisit until the next day I replied: "I felt I could not trust you — that's why I cam earlier." I don't believe she tried a second time to cheat me!

In one case I had to act even more strongly: a man suffering from obstructed hernia refused my advice to go to hospital for an operation. We argued for some time but he maintained: "Whatever you say Doctor, I shall stay here." Knowing that it was a question of life or death I eventually said: "You won't stay here; you will either go to hospital or to the cemetery — the choice is yours." "If that is the position I give in," the man replied and consented to the operation. He came back home cured, a healthy and grateful man, and our relationship remained good.

This happy relationship with my patients also enabled me to put over my opinion in the delicate fields of contraception and abortion. I usually said to the patient: "You may think or have been told that I am against these things because I am a Catholic, but actually I am a Catholic because I believe in these things." I would enlarge on the ill-effects of the "pill" and also the danger of sterilisation,

132

which become more and more known the longer they are employed. As to abortion I pointed out — illustrated by pictures — how the unborn child is already an individual in its own right, and I also told them about the ill-effects, frequently encountered, both physical and psychological. Of course some did not take my advice and though I did not refer them to anybody I made it clear that I could not — and would not — stand in their way. More than one later returned to me asking if I would take them on again as patients, they would not go near the doctor who had "helped" them with the abortion — a fact that, to me, seemed significant.

Practising medicine as I felt, and still feel, it should be done, did not leave me much time for private life. All the same, during those years I developed two of my interests which I kept up ever after. One was in the medico-legal field. No doctor can always avoid being called to Court to give evidence in a case in which one of his patients is involved, and when it happened to me I felt that I cut a very poor figure. The Court does not appreciate that a doctor's diagnosis is largely based on the history and, according to the law, history is hearsay evidence. So of course I got into trouble when I mentioned the medical history. "This is hearsay evidence, you must not say that Doctor," and a short time later I was again warned by the judge: "I have told you already Doctor, your remarks are not admissable as evidence." Opposing Counsel was quick to seize his advantage and soon I was made to feel that I was either considered totally ignorant or dishonest or both. However, when I saw that Counsel for the defence and Counsel for the prosecution were also not always polite to each other but then went more or less arm-in-arm to lunch during the break, I decided this was very much like a game of chess, at which during my youth I had been quite good. I therefore decided to learn the "game" properly, joined the Police Surgeons Association, and since seem to have been successful in this field, which I found more and more absorbing. Ever since 1946, when I started my police work, I dealt increasingly with such cases and in 1956 when after a lapse of many years the appointment of Police Surgeons was reintroduced, I was officially appointed.

My other interest was in the medico-moral field, which gained increasing importance for the Church. At that time Buckfast Abbey published a quarterly "Chronicle" to which I contributed articles, and in consequence I was asked to talk at the Ramsgate Discussion Week which was established by the joint efforts of George Laurence, the head of a private school, and Patricia Hall, a fervent Catholic of wide vision and an amazing gift and energy for organisation. It was she who introduced me to that summer school for young people. It had, as its main theme, "Living to the full" viewed from every angle, but of course plenty of time was given for relaxation and social events. I became a regular participant and it was out of the talks I gave there that more articles were born and eventually the publication of several books followed. I assume that it was in consequence of my published works that I was honoured in 1964 by being created a Knight of the Holy Sepulchre, one of the old Papal Orders of knighthood, and later promoted to a Knight Commander. I therefore owe a lot to Pat Hall, and though she

Our family in front of our house in 1956.

always remained in the background we always kept — and still keep — in touch.

It is many years since I was an enthusiastic traveller. In our young days in Vienna we had regular holidays, mainly abroad, but after the war — while the children were small — we made few journeys. When I took leave it was usually during school time, when the children were in their boarding schools.

Anyway, we had not the money for expensive holidays and so my wife and I took them, if any, without the children. Our first priority was to send the children to good boarding schools. Having ourselves been brought up abroad we were not familiar with the teaching here and, therefore, could not have helped the children with school work. Moreover, we wished that they should grow up feeling from the onset that this was their home country, and without the accent which, of course, my wife and I never lost. In this we succeeded to such an extent that, though they now live largely among Americans, they all cling to their British citizenship and jealously preserve their English accents.

The girls went to convents, and our son first to the Ramsgate Abbey preparatory school and then to Downside. Even though we were given some reduction of fees as long as we needed it, this still left us very short of funds. However, we thought that it was really best for the children to have family life during their vacations rather than travel with us, and it seems we made the right choice; they remained attached to us and to each other, and as to travelling they made up for it later on. Our eldest daughter Gabriele trained as a nurse at my old hospital Westminster, and later was for four years a Royal Air Force sister and as such posted to the RAF Hospital in Aden for two years. When her short service commission came to an end she left the RAF and took an additional Health Visitor's diploma in London, then joined the SSAFA service as a nursing sister. She loved travelling and she loved working with the Forces, and this gave her the opportunity to keep up with both at the same time, having more freedom than in the RAF where she had been under the discipline of a matron and where rules forbade mixing with other ranks. It was in Tripoli that Gabriele met her husband, Bernard Mackenzie, a geophysicist working there though he had been born in Kent only about an hour's journey from where we lived. He is now based in Texas but with his family has travelled all over the world. We were particularly happy when one of his "overseas appointments" was in England for four years. They now have three children, and though they were living on the other side of London we could, for that time, enjoy to some extent a wider family life.

Our son Francis worked on the railways in traffic management, but then felt a vocation to the priesthood and entered a seminary. However, he also felt strongly drawn to social work, and as our then Bishop did not permit him to combine the two things, he asked for and received dispensation from the priesthood vows and became a probation officer. During that time he married a Dutch girl and they now have two boys. However, happy as he was in his appointment and marriage, after a time he evidently missed the ministry, and with the churches having come closer, he decided to become an Anglican. He applied for part-time work, and, after some interviews, having been accepted, helped in his

In the robes of the Order of the Holy Sepulchre, 1964.

local parish church while continuing with probation work. However, the call to the ministry seemed to become ever stronger and he then got an appointment as second chaplain to the English speaking community in The Hague, where he seems perfectly happy. So does his wife who, of course, is at home in that country. During the years on the railway and afterwards, Francis travelled extensively visiting his sisters and friends, and now his work occasionally takes him all over the continent.

Veronica, our younger daughter, trained as a secretary. When she had completed her course she asked if she could go for a year to the United States. "At 18 and as a beginner I won't get much of a job here," she said, and she thought it was a good opportunity to see something of the world and get experience elsewhere. We consented on condition that she lived with a family, which was arranged. When the year came to an end she wrote that she had got a scholarship to one of the colleges and would like to stay another year, at the end of which she asked for yet another year to continue her studies, but married the professor who taught her. Besides having been a professor of mathematics he was an electronics consultant. After their marriage they at first lived in the country in the state of New York, but later he took an appointment in Israel where they stayed for several years. They are now back in the United States but this time in Kentucky and have nine children of their own, besides the two children, by now almost grown up, from her husband's first marriage.

Our elder daughter is a practising Catholic and after many years of marriage her husband followed her into the Church. Our son was followed by his family into the Anglican Church, and Veronica is married to a Jew and celebrates the holidays of both denominations. With this and, at present, fourteen grandchildren, I feel like Abraham "the father of many nations", but with the family widely spread we do not see much of the children and grand-children. However, we are fortunate in that all the marriages seem to be very happy and our in-law children fit into our family very well.

My wife likes travelling but I myself need a strong motivation for it. Thus in 1950 I felt that I should visit my mother in Austria. I managed to persuade her to meet us in Salzburg rather than us going to Vienna, for which the closeness of the Russians gave a ready excuse, although I actually had two reasons of my own for that proposal. My memories of our last days in Vienna were not happy ones, whilst Salzburg always had a special place in my heart. Also, warned by a letter from my mother after her return to Vienna in which she wrote that at the airport she and her brother fell into each other's arms with a shout of joy, I was rather frightened of an emotional scene on the son's homecoming; I did not feel at all that it was a homecoming for me.

Due to the war I had not become a naturalized British citizen until 1947 and subsequently had my name anglicised. The immediate reason for this alteration of our name was a remark of the headmaster when our son entered prep-school: "We cannot call him that all day," he said. It was on the advice of the Colles that we chose the shortening of Pollaczek to Pole, which Hester said with a smile, "had always a great, if not always good, Catholic reputation" in this country. Though the official documentation was therefore fairly recent I had felt at home in England for a long time, and did not at all relish the prospect of a journey into the estranged past. Thus it was in an endeavour to keep my mother's emotions under control that my wife and I did not travel on our own but took Ngaire Porterfield with us. The two had always got on well and Ngaire's presence ensured that our talking would nearly all be in English, thus preventing too much emotion being shown.

My mother seemed to enjoy the stay in Salzburg and appeared to be reasonably well, but soon afterwards her health deteriorated rapidly, and she died of cancer which, undetected, had evidently been present for some time.

We did that journey by road, the last time I drove on the Continent. We took in a visit to our cousins in Lugano where we had stayed on our first journey to England. Unforgettable to me is the drive through two Swiss passes (Maloja and Julier). They had only just been cleared and from the summer weather in Lugano we drove up between walls of snow on each side, and then down again through the melting snow forming rivulets and so, as it were, through all the seasons until we arrived again in the valley with its summer weather.

Another holiday journey took us again to Lugano, this time taking our son, then about 12 years old, with us. Whilst my wife stayed with our cousins I took him on to Venice which I have always loved and which I wanted to show him. I have since been once more to Venice with my wife and though it was very enjoyable and the hotel (Gabrieli-Sandwirth) particularly pleasant and comfortable, I could not help seeing and feeling sad at the considerable decay of this beautiful city over the years I knew it. It was only at night, in the floodlit darkness, that the piazza San Marco re-exerted its magical charm.

Another very special holiday was in 1967 in Tripoli to visit Gabriele. At the time of our visit Gabriele had been married about two-and-a-half years and our eldest grand-daughter was about eighteen months old. It was my first experience of the Orient which I certainly found to be a different world. During the visit we were taken to Sabratha and Leptis Magna, the beautiful and famous ruins of Roman days. But as happens so often the most lasting impression is of everyday life there; the then sandy roads with many wells at the roadside worked by donkeys or camels, and of a donkey cart or an occasional lorry with a camel sitting in it. I was told that camels were not allowed on the roads in the town itself and therefore they were often driven across; it was a very strange sight.

In 1972 we went to Nuremberg where my wife and I were the guests of the Catholic Medical Guild. I had been invited as the main speaker from Britain to talk at the European Congress on "The Doctor's Role in Sex Education". The hospitality we received was quite exceptional, and when the conference was over we extended our journey to visit Rome and once again Salzburg.

Rome is another experience of a lifetime but unfortunately we were pressed for time. My wife had been twice before, and so we confined ourselves to the essentials of secular past and ecclesiastical present. Much as I was impressed by

138

the many wonderful sights, I found the noisy traffic of Rome disturbing and tiring, and in stark contrast to Venice where all traffic moves on water and the noise is only that of human voices.

Probably in consequence of the Nuremberg European Congress I was again asked to read a paper at the International Congress of Catholic Doctors in Washington in 1974. I had once before spoken at the International Congress held in London in 1962 on the problems of "The Hopeless Case". This time I prepared a paper on "Euthanasia", but eventually found that I was unable to attend and my paper was read for me by a colleague; it was afterwards published. The reason I could not go was that I had arranged for my wife and me to take part in a pilgrimage to the Holy Land arranged by the Order of the Holy Sepulchre and I found that I could neither afford the time nor the money to do both. The Holy Land journey obviously took precedence. It is the dream of every Christian to see the Holy Land for himself, and in my particular case I felt that I should know what I was supposed to defend as a Knight! With the political situation being so uncertain nobody was able to foresee when the Order would be able to arrange another pilgrimage, and by now being well over 70, I had to be aware that such a strenuous journey might soon be beyond me.

I was well pleased with my decision. The experience was unforgettable. Being a group of people with the same outlook on life, and most of us either knowing each other or at least knowing of each other, with two exceptional priests, Mgr Peter Strand and Father Kevin Kenny, as spiritual directors, and with the same guide during the whole journey, all commercialism was kept away from us. Whenever one has such a series of marvellous experiences, one stands out in particular and for me it was Mass in the manger chapel. The one and only disappointment on the journey was the Garden of Gethsemane, which is divided up between various Christian denominations, with churches in between, and the Catholic part is now just a very small garden which makes it impossible to have a really vivid picture of the happenings there as recounted in the gospels. This stark evidence of the divisions in the Christian faith and the lack of compliance with Christ's teaching that all should be one, filled us with sadness.

At the end of the pilgrimage we stayed behind to spend a few days with our younger daughter Veronica, who lived in Israel at that time with four children.

In the years between these journeys I spent my holidays mainly attending the Police Surgeons' Annual Conferences — one of them abroad in Amsterdam — and spending some time quietly at Buckfast Abbey. My wife came to the Conference with me, and when I stayed at the Abbey she usually stopped at the guest house or with friends in the neighbourhood.

My thriving practice and the police work, which steadily grew, soon made it necessary for me to have a secretary, and this in turn enabled me to increase my activities, giving talks at schools to pupils in the top forms, to Parent-Teacher Associations, as Medical Adviser to the Catholic Advisory Marriage Centre, as an officer in the Guild of Catholic Doctors, in the Catenians — an association of Catholic professional men and businessmen — as Corps Surgeon in the St John Ambulance Brigade which I joined when the Home Guard was finally disbanded,

Bernard and Jean Flavin with Francis and me on a tour, visiting Abbot Upson at Prinknash Abbey.

and eventually also as a council member in the Police Surgeons Association. Whilst, therefore, my secretary originally acted mainly as a receptionist and filing clerk, and keeping the surgery and equipment in order, the field of her activities gradually increased, and with it my demands on her capabilities. There were three or four who could not keep pace and soon dropped out of my employment, but I was later lucky that the wife of a police sergeant friend of mine volunteered to help me out when I was temporarily without a secretary, and, as it turned out, she stayed with me for two-and-a-half years until, in 1958, he got an appointment as a rural sergeant and they moved from our district. We are still great friends with the Flavins.

That year, 1958, brought a great change in my life. The house where we lived was paid for and the neighbouring house came on the market. It was a very nice, detached house and for a long time I had had my eye on it for a surgery, but could not afford it when it was previously up for sale. Now I still could not really afford it, and moreover it was the time of the first big credit squeeze on the banks. Still I took courage in both hands, and went to my bank manager, who was a patient of mine and whom I knew to be friendly and sympathetic. However, I hardly dared hope he would be as helpful as he turned out to be.

"How much money will you need?" he asked, and seemed rather surprised when I said: "105% of the purchase price." I explained that the money I had saved was needed for the alterations necessary to make the house where we lived into a real family home, and the new house into the surgery of my dreams. "How

25 and 27 South Avenue (the latter had just become my property for the Surgery) 1958.

will you pay back?" was the next question. "I don't know," I answered truthfully, "Probably nothing for two years, but the bank can have the whole sum in ten years when my life-endowment policy matures, which will provide full cover." Mr Willey, the bank manager, came to see the house and decided that to anybody it was worth the money I intended paying for it, and to me it was a bargain. My neighbours, who then lived in the house were also patients of mine, they knew they were leaving the house in the spring, and they too were very helpful. "Go ahead, I shall get you the money somehow," said the manager, "But it is too early to speak to the directors about it." He rang me again in the spring. "I go tomorrow to see the directors," he said, "and shall tell them I have to hang myself if they don't give you the money because I promised it to you." I got the money, and on April 1st 1958 I took over the house. Ten weeks later I opened my surgery there, which was just what I had always wanted. It comprised, besides the comfortable waiting room, a consulting room furnished as a sitting room where I could get the patients to relax and talk, a clinically equipped examination-treatment room and, of course, a separate office. Two rooms, a kitchen and a bathroom upstairs served as a caretaker's flat.

My secretary, whom I have mentioned before, had just left and for a few weeks I had temporary help who, however, was unable to undertake the task permanently. Then, through a patient of mine, I was put in contact with Mrs Fox, who had been a solicitor's secretary; she had not worked for a few years but kept up her shorthand and typing. Her daughter was, by now, 13 years old

141

Peggy and Bob Fox with their daughter Jenny.

which allowed mother to take a part-time job. We quickly agreed on arrangements subject to this daughter's approval, a condition her mother made which I particularly liked. Jenny, the daughter, came to view me and the place; we got on very well and she said: "Mummy take the job." For my part, I invited her that, whenever she left school early before mother got home, she could find a quiet corner in the office to do her homework.

Jean, my former long-term secretary, came back for a few days to show Peggy Fox the ropes concerning the few things she had not done before, like the maintenance and sterilising of instruments. The surgery was particularly full in those

Dr Kain Bhat

days with patients being curious to see the new house. It was only much later, when Peggy and I had become friends and not just boss and secretary, that she confided to me that, on the first evening she wrote to her husband (who was then at sea with the Royal Fleet Auxiliary): "This place is a mad house, I won't last a week." She remained with me for almost twenty-three years until her death in April 1981.

All the time I had satisfactory relief arrangements for holidays and days off, which enabled me to keep up my various other non-practice activities. However, in 1962 difficulties arose and I decided to take a partner. At first I had Michael Sykes, a very nice young doctor, a friend of our elder daughter, who was very popular with the patients, but he favoured the new ideas of group practices and rotas with neighbouring practices for days and nights off and free weekends. This I did not consent to, and after a few months we parted. We remained on good terms but he moved with his family to the seaside as a partner in a group practice.

I was again fortunate in quickly finding another partner, Kain Bhat, a highly qualified young Indian with an English wife. They are still friends of ours, and he my doctor. From the very beginning I made arrangements with him that we would not join a rota, that we would remain just the two of us relieving each other for time off, and in return for his complying with my wishes I promised to retire by the end of 1967 on my 65th birthday from National Health Service practice, and leave him all the patients, while I intended to carry on private practice.

My wife's parents with their two eldest great grandchildren, Michelle and
Philippa on holiday with us in 1970.

Chapter 14
PRIVATE PRACTICE AND POLICE WORK

It was a leap in the dark — nobody could foresee if I would be able to build up a private practice sufficiently large to at least maintain itself, but I was determined to chance it. Group practices and rota arrangements became more and more common in those days and I did not feel that my strong individualism would fit into either. On the other hand I knew that I could not keep my partner happy outside such arrangments beyond the originally stipulated time. After some friendly discussion we decided that I would keep the surgery house and try to make it pay by private practice, and the Police Surgeon's job, while he bought a bungalow round the corner to continue National Health Service practice there.

It all worked out as planned. Many of my former National Health Service patients remained with me as private patients and recommendations quickly increased the size of my practice. I enjoyed giving more time and making closer personal contacts with my patients, though in essence I did not — and could not — treat them any better than I had done under the NHS; I was also able to increase my surgical activities for which I always retained a special liking. As I had kept friendly with all the doctors in the district over the years, some of them now increasingly referred patients to me for small operations for which a consultant's fee would have been much higher. In spite of this I also remained friendly with the surgeons, particularly one who occasionally asked me to assist him at private operations. A little later, when his anaesthetist died, John Hill, a local dental surgeon asked me to be his anaesthetist for regular sessions twice a week. The Police Surgeon's work increased year by year with the growth of crime and also with neighbouring police divisions sending special cases to me, in which their own, much younger police surgeons had not yet much experience.

When I was approved under Section 28 of the Mental Health Act as a doctor with special experience in the diagnosis or treatment of mental illness, the Social Services sent such cases with increased frequency to me, and I then also got higher fees for them than before — the same actually as a consultant.

Thus I did very well, building up an unusually large private practice until, when I reached the age of 75, I felt that work was becoming too much, and I consequently retired from general practice on that birthday. I only kept on my work as police surgeon and for the Social Services who referred to me besides mental emergencies, mainly non-accidental injuries to children. Some of those were among my police cases.

When I closed down my surgery I moved with my wife into the former surgery house. Up to then I had examined major police cases — particularly sex offences — in my own place, as the rooms provided in the operational stations, used for the routine cases of drinking drivers, prisoners and various minor injuries, were too small and not equipped — nor could be — for more intricate examinations. It was then that Chief Superintendent Harold Pattison — at that time head of our B-Division — gave me suitable accommodation in the old Gillingham Police Station which was no longer operational but housed various departmental offices. I got a suite consisting of a small anteroom, which I share with the Special Branch of the Police and from which there are separate doors into a waiting-interview room, an examination room and a cubby hole for the storage of files, drugs, spare dressings, etc. . . . The rooms are equipped with my former surgery furniture and instruments, and provide one of the best facilities in the country which led to the layout being published under the title "A Police Surgeon's Suite in Kent" in the autumn issue of the supplement to the Police Surgeons' Journal.

If my present work takes up a disproportionate part of this book, it does so for a good reason. I am very fond of the police work and all that is connected with it and I find that people have a very wrong impression of what it involves. Time and again I have been asked by doctors and others if it is not terrible to get up in the night to take blood from a drinking-driver. It seems that the impression prevails that this is all the police surgeon does, but actually — though the largest single item — it comprises on average only about 40% of my work and only half the work is at night. With an average of some four hundred cases a year, that leaves still plenty of other often fascinating cases for me to deal with. In many of them I have to examine several people, as in a murder or rape where all suspects have to be screened; all these examinations are counted as the same case. On the other hand, if one man commits more than one offence, as for example injuring several police officers, each examination — representing a possible charge — is counted as a separate case.

I am certainly very fortunate in that the prospect of possibly being awoken at night (some three to four times a week) does not keep me awake, and I still have the capacity of my young days to go to sleep within about five minutes of my return to bed, whatever the case was that had called me out.

The work the police surgeon does is very much a doctor's work, concerned with personal relationships and professional ethics like any other but also with the criminal law and justice. I have already explained how I became a police surgeon and I have never regretted it. To have one's findings and opinions scrutinised by solicitors is a particular challenge. In his reports, the police surgeon must be very careful not to over-step his competence. Knowing the history, findings will be described as compatible with, suggestive of or incompatible with, but very rarely as conclusive. A full report anticipating as many as possible of the questions which may arise will often save a Court attendance.

Even if no report is required a full aide memoir must be kept. One can never foresee all the questions that may arise often many months later. I well remember the case of a prisoner to whom I was called because he was suffering from migraine. He told me he had been given tablets by his doctor but they "were no good" so he left them off. Evidently they had helped after all, because now he had a migraine attack worse than for a very long time. Many months later I had a telephone call from a solicitor telling me that he was defending the man against a charge of theft, and he was told that I had been called to examine him because he had been injured while in custody. I looked up my aide memoire and rang back the solicitor to say I could only let him have a full report with the consent of the police as I had examined the man on their behalf, but I did not think the report would make him very happy. I did not hear anything further until one day I was telephoned by the police asking if I could attend Court that afternoon. I could not and was under no obligation to do so as I had had no previous warning, but I suggested I would submit a written statement. This was accepted, and in it I explained that I had treated the man for migraine and no allegations of injuries were made at the time, nor were any found. I was later told that after counsel for both sides had read my statement the allegations against the police were not mooted in Court and the case was dealt with in the ordinary way.

When called to Court a doctor often faces a difficult time under cross-examination and that was particularly so before the introduction of blood and/or urine tests, when he had to defend his conclusions in a drinking-driver case. This may be illustrated by a probably spurious but characteristic story which was jocularly bandied about some years ago. According to it, counsel asked the doctor: "How long did it take you to examine the defendant?" "Three-quarters of an hour," replied the doctor. "That is rather a long time," was the retort, "Doesn't it show that you were very doubtful in your own mind?" A week later the same doctor and the same solicitor met again in Court on a similar case. "How long did it take you to examine the defendant?" "A quarter of an hour," said the doctor. "Isn't that rather short?" came the retort, "I suggest it shows that you had made up your mind beforehand."

The phrase "it is obvious you have made up your mind that the accused should be convicted" is one I met myself in a case where opposing counsel could not get me to change my evidence and opinion. "The question of conviction does not concern me. Good luck to anybody who can prove his innocence," was my reply. "But of course I have made up my mind what the findings mean. After all, this is my task and I had plenty of time to do so." Whereupon counsel sat down — no more questions. Evidently he had hoped I would say that I had not made up my mind, which would have given him the opportunity to say: "Oh doctor you admit you have not yet made up your mind about the case."

Now that I have got used to Court proceedings I am always treated politely and often with respect. In the rare cases where opposing counsel tries to cut me short by saying: "Doctor, just answer yes or no," I appeal to the judge or chairman, explaining: "As the question is put the answer is yes (or no) but this might be misleading and after all I am sworn to tell the whole truth." In this way I have always succeeded in putting my case.

Drinking-driver cases now rarely require the attendance of the doctor in Court, except when the taking of a specimen for laboratory tests has been refused and the question arises whether such refusal was justified or unjustified. There are, however, still cases charged under the Section of the Road Traffic Act as driving under the influence of drink and/or drugs to such an extent that his ability to drive properly was for the time being impaired, which require a full examination and may be disputed in Court.

Prisoners arrested for drug offences of any kind may actually present considerable problems. A person found drunk and incapable has committed an offence, but to be drugged and incapable is no offence except if one of the restricted drugs is found in his possession. This means that if the person detained regains consciousness, nothing further can be done to help him except if he voluntarily agrees. If drugs are found in the possession of a prisoner, they can usually be identified with some certainty but still have to be sent to the laboratory to have the provisional diagnosis confirmed. I remember the case of one prisoner who denied that the drugs were his and alleged they had been planted on him by the police. I thereupon suggested a urine test which he could not very well decline, and when as expected it was returned positive nothing more was heard of that allegation. One of the most dangerous drugs, because of its possibly long-lasting after-effects, is LSD, and this of course belongs to the drugs on the restricted list. In my opinion, however, almost equally dangerous are the barbitones, particularly if tablets meant for swallowing are dissolved and injected. According to the present law, whoever dispenses barbitones without prescription commits an offence, but not so the user. If a preparation meant for oral use is injected, the danger to health and limb because of infection and thrombosis is added to that of the action of barbitones.

Some people advocate that cannabis should be legalised as it presents only a small danger to the user's health. In my opinion this argument is wrong, because cannabis is certainly one of those drugs which causes divorce from reality; this always means danger, particularly on the road, whether as driver or pedestrian, by not seeing what is there or by seeing what is not there. If ever cannabis is legalised its use would have to be confined to special places only (like the opium dens in the East!) if catastrophes are to be avoided.

Even cases where alcohol is the only drug involved may engage considerable human interest. Blood can only be taken with the consent of the suspect, and this applies even to ordinary clinical examination. If a person is drunk and incapable to such an extent that he can neither give nor refuse consent, the police surgeon has to examine him clinically for his own safety but, of course, not give the police any information beyond the fact that he is unfit to drive (if this applies) and fit or unfit to be detained. The prisoner has to be considered as a patient and therefore the rule of medical confidentiality applies. In one such case many years ago I accordingly told the police inspector: "The man is fit to be detained but unfit to drive. Why, I cannot tell you." "What do you mean? You can't tell me?" "Well, I haven't the man's permission to tell you." "You can't grow old without growing artful," was the inspector's smiling reply; next morning the prisoner gave me the required permission being certainly quite aware that nobody had any doubt what had caused his condition.

Drivers cannot be too strongly warned that they should never rely on their capability to drive well even if they have drunk a little more than comes within the legal limit and, that, therefore, they will escape the attention of the police. After any accident, breath tests are taken from both drivers and I remember a particularly sad case. The person causing the accident — and with it severe injuries to the passengers in the other car — was convicted of dangerous driving, but the innocent man still lost his licence because his blood showed more than the permitted level of alcohol.

Regarding breath tests, they are at present only screening tests which justify a driver's being taken to the police station for a blood test. Replacement of blood tests with new breath test machines, which give a reading on the spot, is now under consideration. Even though the new instruments are supposed to be accurate, the readings will never be as reliable as blood tests. If just previous to the breath test the driver has belched, thus bringing some of the stomach alcohol into the mouth, the reading will be too high. The same may happen if some food is trapped under the dentures and has soaked up some of the drink which, on the forceful breathing into the breath test apparatus, will be dislodged into it. Such apparatus may well cut down the number of blood tests because a driver who feels guilty is likely to avoid further expense and accept the reading as true. However there will always have to be provision made for those who feel that the reading is too high, and demand a blood test. The facts of the consequent reduction in the number of blood tests and the driver himself having requested it in each case, which will invariably make him co-operative, will certainly lighten the burden on the police surgeon, but I doubt that this will justify the considerable expense of purchasing and maintaining those instruments, while under the present arrangements any expense can be added to the fine of the driver who is found guilty.

Examination of prisoners may be required by the police or the prisoner himself under many varied circumstances.

Some prisoners may complain of illness and/or pain, others may have been injured in an affray or even at work before arrest and need treatment, and it is a question of fitness to be detained. Some others may have injured themselves in committing their offences like cut wounds sustained in break-ins or criminal damage, and the description of their injuries and grouping of the blood may serve as evidence, while in some cases they claim that the police have inflicted an injury and they want to complain. In the last mentioned cases, the records of the examination have to be very thorough and I always read aloud the record of my findings to the prisoner, so that he has a chance to say his own piece. If there are real injuries it is up to the policeman to justify why he could not help injuring the prisoner, which often happens in resisting arrest. I frequently find that I have to examine more than one injured police officer, in a case of injury to a prisoner. But in any case my examination is completely impartial and must be seen to be so.

Unfortunately, violence is considerably on the increase, not only pub fights but also muggings, robbery with violence and non-accidental injuries to wives and children. The last mentioned sometimes come to me through the Social

Services departments and sometimes through the police. They can present a particularly difficult problem if accidental and non-accidental injuries are both present, as in the case of a child where the mother had inflicted cigarette burns and the child had also sustained other injuries in a fight with his brother.

After having been overlooked for many years, injuries to children are today almost all too often suspected of being non-accidental, but it must not be forgotten that accidents can still happen even under the most unusual circumstances. In one such case, a woman had been told that she could not have a child herself and she and her husband managed to get one for adoption which was brought up so well that she was allowed to foster a second one with view to adoption. During the time of fostering she found that she was expecting a baby of her own, but had become very attached to the child and still wanted to adopt it. She had been such a good adoptive mother that her plea was accepted. "One cannot send a baby one has grown fond of back like a parcel," she said. Then one day, with the baby in her arms, she slipped on the floor where the dog had spilt his food, and the child's head crashed against the table. They nursed him and put him to bed, but got alarmed when the baby, on waking, refused food, and they called me. The circumstances appeared classical of a battered baby syndrome, but the couple had been patients of mine for many years, I knew them well and was convinced it was an accident. The baby died and post-mortem examination confirmed that death was due to a fractured skull in an otherwise perfectly healthy baby, and the inquest ended with a verdict of "accidental death" with the natural mother and the foster mother comforting each other and the coroner comforting them both.

In robbery cases the question might arise as to what weapon had been used, and in one case of attempted mugging it was the assailant and not the intended victim who came off worst. The 64-year-old man, who had been a boxer, laid out the assailant on the floor of a public lavatory, where he still was when the police, whom he had called, arrived. Quite coolly he observed: "I'm glad he didn't assault an old age pensioner, he might not have been able to cope."

In many cases of assault the police surgeon's attendance in Court is required and often there is a stringent cross-examination. In one case of robbery an old man was hit, I thought with the side of a fist, to push him out of the way. "Doctor, what makes you say it was a fist blow?" I was asked. "Well, the shape and size seemed to fit, it was something roundish, not very hard and with a fair violence, certainly enough to make the man fall into a nearby chair," was my reply. "Couldn't it have been anything else?" "Being not very hard and rounded it could, of course, have been a tennis ball thrown by a child", was my further reply. It was evident that this possibility did not fit the occasion and no further questions were asked. Another case was one of an injured police officer, where again I thought it was a fist blow, but this time with a circumscribed centre which I thought was due to a knuckle. "It could, of course, have been anything else doctor." "Well, it could have been a ring making the mark." "Of course it could have been anything else," repeated counsel. It was probably against the strict rules of the Court that I addressed my reply not to the jury but to counsel direct. "I can't think of anything else, can you?" It seems counsel too had no other suggestions because no further questions were asked.

Difficulties may arise over the age of injuries, which it is often impossible to tell, though the relative age of two sets can usually be established. In one such case a man in a pub had pushed his beer glass into the face of another man and the glass broke in his hands, thus cutting the face of the victim and the attacker's hand. The assailant promptly ran off but when he was found two days after, he resisted arrest and received superficial injuries. On examination I found cuts and scratches, and he then claimed they all dated from the scuffle with the police that evening. However, it was clear that only some were fresh and others older, compatible with having been sustained by broken glass two days previously. I was able to make that clear, even to the accused, who said, somewhat ruefully: "One can see which side you are on," but thereafter pleaded guilty.

Every sudden, unexpected death has to be seen by a doctor before the body can be moved, and such deaths are a fairly frequent reason for the police surgeon to be called. Sometimes this happens just because the family doctor is not available and there are no suspicious circumstances attached to it. In others, there are suspicious circumstances and the police surgeon has to decide whether this is likely to be a case due to natural causes, to suicide, accident or foul play. If foul play is suspected the Home Office pathologist is called, but even then both the police and the Home Office pathologist will allow an experienced police surgeon, whom they have known for some time, to deal with everything at the scene of suspected crime, the Home Office pathologist performing the post-mortem examination afterwards.

The picture the scene presents can be deceiving, as in a case where a woman was found dead in a small pool of blood around her head, lying on a carpeted floor, with blood marks along the hallway, on the door and the wall of the room where she was found. Life was obviously extinct, and after photographs had been taken the officer in charge of the case gave his consent that I could do a further examination. I found no sign of foul play, the blood had come from the nose, and when I told the officer that I thought it was a case of natural death he enquired further into the circumstances and the following story emerged: the aged woman had had a nose bleed in the hallway, felt faint and the even older husband supported her walking into the room. However, she got heavier and heavier for him and he braced himself against the door and the walls leaving marks from his hands which had been stained by the blood from the nose. In the end he had to let her slide to the floor and, as the post-mortem examination confirmed, she died there from a coronary thrombosis. In another case a man who died from a stroke had at first fallen against a chair, the chair against the table, they both were knocked over, and things lying on the table had fallen to the ground. The whole room looked at first sight as if a fight had taken place, suggesting foul play, but further examination showed no other signs of it and the post-mortem examination confirmed that death was due to a cerebral haemorrhage.

Shooting and hanging cases may be difficult to analyse. Of the latter I remember one of suicide in which the hands had been tied behind the back with a sliding knot, one due to accident with a practical joke having gone wrong, and two at least where death occurred accidentally during perverse sexual experiments. Very well known is a case of initially unsuspected murder with which the late Professor Camps dealt. An army sergeant was killed by a karate blow and then hung up to simulate suicide. It might have been passed as such had the man who committed the crime not married the widow and set the people talking, which led to exhumation and a second post-mortem revealing the real cause.

Even in cases of seeming natural death, the doctor cannot be too careful as Dr Havard pointed out in his book on "Secret Homicide". Even a hopeless illness need not be the cause of death, relatives may have got tired of nursing the invalid and "hastened death".

In cases of suspected murder, the police surgeon as a member of the investigating team will help at the scene of the crime, and also examine the victim and any suspect, particularly for any injuries he himself received and as to his mental state.

Sex offences are not always of a violent nature. In a great number of cases, girls between the ages of 14 and 16 are involved who were very willing partners, though in law their consent is not valid. Unfortunately the age group seems to get younger and younger, some cases occur within the family and may amount to incest, some are cases of rape or attempted rape. The cases become known because young girls are missing and return home under circumstances which are suspect of a sexual offence having taken place, and though often the girls do not find anything wrong with it and consider the examination as interference with their private lives and decisions, they usually submit to the examination without difficulty. In some cases they object: "Why pick on me, Ann, Mary and Jackie have done the same," and in following this up more cases come to light. Consequently such examinations may occur in groups, as also offences against small boys.

Sometimes girls are actually proud of their sexual experience, as in the case of three schoolgirls who freely admitted to having had intercourse. In two of them examination confirmed what they had said, but the third girl was a virgin and when this was put to her admitted that she had not had intercourse but confessed to it because she did not want to be the odd one out, who would be laughed at by the others. In one very unusual case, two girls of 9 and 11 actually provoked the offence by flouncing in front of a mentally retarded young fellow. The younger watched first and then said: "I want the same." When the young man hesitated, not feeling up to it, she said: "If you don't I shall tell Mummy what you did to Betty." He could not oblige and she told Mummy!

Most cases with children, however, do not amount to intercourse but to indecent assault only, and if the case is examined soon enough after the offence, it will usually reveal evidence.

In order to establish rape it is not sufficient for the police surgeon to find signs of intercourse having taken place, but there must also be some proof of unwilling participation on the part of the victim. There may be signs of violence or defence wounds, as in the case of one woman in whom a small slit in the back of the dress and the slight mark of a knife point confirmed her story that she had given in under threat of violence. However, even violence may not always prove the case. A young woman was found tied to a bed half dead from strangulation, and the circumstances seemed to support her allegation that she had been raped, though locally there was no injury, but only evidence of recent intercourse. However, when the assailant was found he stated that intercourse had taken place with the girl's consent, but during intercourse she reminded him so much of his wife — who had deserted him — that fury overcame him and he decided to murder her. He actually thought he had done so. He said he was willing to plead guilty to attempted murder but did not want it said that he was a sex maniac who raped girls. The man's evidence was accepted in Court. As a matter of fact his story had a truer ring than her's, as she had no satisfactory explanation why, at the end of a party held in his flat, she returned to it when the other guests had left. The sentence for attempted murder was almost certainly no less than that for rape would have been; thus the accused did not benefit in this respect but honour was preserved.

In other cases, though the explanation of the assailant is very plausible, it may be untrue. A doctor friend of mine was in Court to give evidence in a case, and having arrived early sat in on the previous one. This concerned a complaint by a young man that in the cinema an elderly man in the front row changed his seat to sit next to him, and then tried to interfere with him manually underneath the overcoat which the assailant had lain across his knees. The accused denied the accusation and said he was suffering from a hernia which had "come out" and which he tried to push back underneath the overcoat; any touching of his neighbour was accidental. Having given his evidence the man fainted and my friend was asked to attend to him while the bench retired to consider their verdict. The examination proved the man's story to be a lie, he had no hernia; however, when the doctor and the accused returned to Court, the bench pronounced that they had accepted the man's evidence and found him not guilty. His lie had saved the man and nothing could be done to avoid a miscarriage of justice. Even if the doctor had returned to Court before the verdict was pronounced she (it was a lady doctor) would not have been entitled to divulge the man's secret, as the examination was not carried out on behalf of the police but for the man's benefit and, therefore, was covered by the doctor's duty of confidentiality.

Though positive evidence is needed for the police surgeon to confirm the diagnosis "rape" that does not mean that allegations in cases where such proof cannot be found are considered to be spurious. In many cases the police surgeon may be convinced that the allegations are true in spite of his negative findings. In every case he will have to listen sympathetically to anything the examinee says and if the assertion of some organisations is true, that sympathy often appears to be lacking, the doctor concerned in the case is not properly qualified for the job. The moment the examinee — may it be victim or suspect — feels that the rapport is unsatisfactory, her or his story becomes distorted or dries up

Peggy (by now my secretary for over 20 years) and I in my new Police Surgeon's room, 1978.

altogether. It is therefore only in the very end, after interview and examination, that I make up my mind on three points: (1) Can I prove the case? (2) Is there anything to support the story which I believe to be true, though I cannot find any definite proof? (3) Are there strong reasons to disbelieve the story. Observation of and notes on the behaviour of the victim as well as of the accused (if known and seen) may in such cases be helpful but it must be remembered that as in any other upsetting experience (of which traffic accidents are a classic example) the patient (and they are to be considered as patients!) may be initially calm and only after a time show signs of distress, while another may be distressed at once and later may or may not regain normal balance. I differ however in my approach from most other police surgeons in that I do not usually take a full case history but accept the statement given to the police and ask only supplementary questions. I consider my task to be that of telling the police if my findings and observations are positive evidence, compatible or incompatible with the story given to them and I fear that I would find myself in difficulties if, on taking a full history, I got a story different from that given to the police; a clash between my duty to the patient not to divulge some information and that as examining police surgeon may well result. I have always found that supplementary questions during a chat while I examine, answer my purpose completely. Of course the police may have some other supportive evidence in cases which don't yield any medical proof on which they can proceed, but those who lack such evidence, though believed, may never come up in Court.

In spite of the assertion of Mrs Margaret Puxon (doctor and barrister) in her address to a meeting of the Medico-Legal Society on January 11th 1979, that she knows of no evidence that a large number of women who complain about being raped are either amoral or lying, such cases are, in my experience, by no means uncommon.

Sometimes allegations of rape are false because of the need to excuse a late return home to the parents or the husband. In one such case a married woman alleged she had been raped by an escort who brought her home from a dance, and though there were no findings of violence there was nothing to contradict her assertion that she had given in to intercourse out of fear. However, when I had just finished my examination she said: "And he had me from the rear as well." Such cases if they are of recent or habitual occurrence leave definite evidence which can be ascertained on medical examination. Finding it missing in this case I put it to her that the allegation was evidently false, and she then admitted that the whole story was a fabrication because she did not want her husband to know she was a willing partner. She was reassured that, of course, her secret would be kept, and when the policewoman who dealt with the case visited the woman next day she found her in bed, the husband sitting at her side comforting her over "the terrible ordeal" she had gone through the previous night.

Allegations are often withdrawn as in the case of a young woman who alleged she had been raped in a shopping centre under circumstances which appeared to make it impossible. In another case a young woman alleged rape in her own bed by a lodger, and said she had been afraid to shout for help though her sister and brother-in-law were sleeping in the room next to hers with their bed on the other side of the same wall. Some malicious allegations occur, not only about rape but also about incest trumped up by wives who are seeking revenge on their husbands for something quite different, or even by daughters "gunning" for their fathers in retaliation for what they think is too strict discipline. Fortunately a thorough medical examination and investigation into the circumstances usually seems to reveal the truth. False allegations of rape by willing partners are nothing new. In the foreword to the Folio edition 1972 of Utopia, Paul Turner quotes Epigrammata, 1520, page 70, No.149, a poem by Thomas More describing a case of rape: the lady protests so much that finally the ravisher loses patience. "Now I warn you," he said, "If you don't shut up and lie down at once, I'm off." Cowed by this fearful threat, the girl immediately lay down. "All right, go ahead," she said, "But remember, you forced me into it." As the principal law officer at the time, Thomas More knew what he was talking about and was certainly not a man given to levity.

Occasionally proof of sexual offence can be supplied not by the police surgeon, but by the laboratory examining the samples. I remember cases in which the sample had nothing at all to do with the doctor. In one of them — not my own case — soil adherent to the boot matched the place of an alleged offence to which the suspect denied having been. However, it was the soil of a railway embankment which had been brought from afar and no other soil in the neighgourhood was of the same type. In other cases, a laundry mark or manufacturer's label led the police to the culprit.

In the cases of sex offences generally considered as "unnatural" the principles of examination and evidence are the same.

Mental cases come to me either through the police or the Social Services departments, mainly at night when the family doctor is not available and the relief service cannot help. Anyway this used to be so while the Social Services were at night on stand-by duty. Now that this is discontinued these cases are almost always dealt with through the police.

Of course I miss the advantages of knowing the details regarding history and environment which the family doctor possesses and mine is therefore a sort of "frontline psychiatry". Many of the cases I thus see are not certifiable, and it often is a question of keeping the patient happy until the morning, when more can be done. In one such case a woman who had just moved from another district had run out of her tablets for a chronic mental condition, and had not yet succeeded in finding a doctor to take her on his NHS list. "Must I break a window in order to get attention?" she asked very sensibly. I assured her there was no need for that, I would find her a doctor in the morning. This I did, and meanwhile we made her as comfortable as we could in the anteroom of the police station. Of course one has always to be on the lookout for malingerers, often vagrants, who are really not ill at all, but searching for a bed for the night.

In consequence of my police work I also sometimes get asked by defence solicitors to give my opinion in cases where I was not involved on behalf of the police, and the police rather welcome it. One of our senior police officers actually told me: "It is good not only to be impartial, but to be seen to be so, and this will be accepted more readily if you are occasionally known to act for the defence."

Another offshoot of my police work was that I became medical adviser to the Medway Victims Support Scheme, born out of the conviction that in these days much is done for the culprit, but too little for the victim.

EPILOGUE

I had always hoped to carry on as a police surgeon as hitherto until the age of 80. However, I fell ill and though I recovered well, if slowly, I realised that old age had caught up with me; no longer did I feel as active and energetic as I had done before, when I got up from bed for police cases three or four times a week in the night and sometimes two or three times in the same night.

Moreover, during my convalescence Peggy, my secretary, fell ill and it soon became obvious that she had only a short time to live. She died at the beginning of April 1981. During her almost 23 years with me, she had accompanied me to most major cases during the day, took the dictation and typed the report there and then, so that the police had at once the full facts in black and white. She also came with me to Court and took notes of my being cross-examined, a fact that often proved useful. In the evenings she took dictation over the telephone and typed out the reports; this was so well known and appreciated that she was even quoted in the Police Surgeons' Journal as "Dr Pole's secretary who does reports at any time between 8 a.m. and 10 p.m." That indeed she did, and would have been willing to do it even longer, but her husband rightly objected to being awoken during the night by the telephone bell.

Her ever-ready help, no doubt, contributed to my popularity for special examinations needing urgent and full reports and how much the police appreciated her is obvious from a letter a detective inspector wrote after her death: "On behalf of all those officers that have in the past benefited from her services as your 'right arm'" and referring to her "dedicated service performed in such a charming and pleasant manner".

I was aware that without her I could not keep up my standard of service, but I was not prepared to lower it and consequently handed in my resignation as Divisional Police Surgeon.

It was a hard decision because I was loath to sever completely my link with the police and my interest in the more puzzling cases — of which there are many — remained as lively as ever. Many friends I had made among the police officers in the years of work together also wanted me to remain available for such special cases, but I could not see how this could be done. To block the appointment of a new, full Divisional Police Surgeon and to expect my deputy and others to carry on with the run-of-the-mill cases on a deputy's pay would have been patently unfair; they had done more for me during my illness and convalescence than their duty and I was very grateful to them.

Great therefore was my joy when, in reply to my letter of resignation, the Chief Constable suggested a solution by offering me the position of Honorary Consultant Police Surgeon to the Kent County Constabulary. It was a singular honour, and expressed in terms most appreciative of the assistance I had given over the many years. I felt I could accept, as the amount of work likely to be involved would be within my capacity, particularly as the police offered to put a secretary at my disposal in the cases I did for them.

Still, what is left of my life, now that I am 79, can only be an epilogue to the two halves of my very active life. However, I hope that even that can be still made worthwhile. In practical terms it will mean being still professionally useful, even if on a diminishing scale, and having more home life — for which working life left all too little time — helping my wife and being helped by her. But, of course, there are other things which might not be immediately and obviously practical, but ultimately even of greater consequence as all practicalities stem from them; these are the thoughts and endeavours given to the "Mysteries of Life and Death".

Meresborough Books

Proprietors Hamish and Barbara Mackay Miller
7 STATION ROAD, RAINHAM, GILLINGHAM, KENT. ME8 7RS
Telephone Medway (0634) 371591

We are a small publisher specialising in books about Kent. Our books are available in most bookshops in the county including our own bookshop at this address. Alternatively you may order direct, adding 10% for post (minimum 20p, orders over £20.00 post free). When quoting ISBN's please add prefix 0 905270.

BYGONE KENT. A monthly journal on all aspects of Kent History. 95p per month. Annual Subscription £10.50. All back numbers to October 1979 available.

HARDBACKS

TWO HALVES OF A LIFE by Doctor Kary Pole. The autobiography of a Viennese doctor who escaped from the Nazis and established a new career in Kent. ISBN 509. £5.95.

SOUTH EAST BRITAIN: ETERNAL BATTLEGROUND by Gregory Blaxland. A complete military history. ISBN 444. £5.95.

THE WHITE HORSE AND THE KANGAROO by Clive W. Porter. A complete record of the cricket matches between Kent and the Australian touring teams, ISBN 312. £5.50.

KENT AIRFIELDS IN THE BATTLE OF BRITAIN by The Kent Aviation Historical Research Society. A study of nine airfields. Over 100 photographs. ISBN 363. £5.95.

HAWKINGE 1912-1961 by Roy Humphreys. An in depth study of the former RAF Station. 100 photographs. ISBN 355. £5.95.

A NEW DICTIONARY OF KENT DIALECT by Alan Major. The first major work on the subject for over 90 years. ISBN 274. £7.50.

KENT CASTLES by John Guy. The first comprehensive guide to all the castles and castle sites in Kent. ISBN 150. £7.50.

US BARGEMEN by A.S. Bennett. A new book of sailing barge life around Kent and Essex from the author of 'June of Rochester' and 'Tide Time'. ISBN 207. £6.95.

THE GILLS by Tony Conway. A history of Gillingham Football Club. 96 large format pages packed with old photographs. ISBN 266. £5.95. BARGAIN OFFER £1.95.

A VIEW OF CHRIST'S COLLEGE, BLACKHEATH by A.E.O. Crombie, B.A., Headmaster and Tutor 1920-1976. ISBN 223. £6.95.

PAPERBACKS

CYCLE TOURS OF KENT by John Guy. No.1: Medway, Gravesend, Sittingbourne and Sheppey. ISBN 517. £1.50.

THE LIFE AND ART OF ONE MAN by Dudley Pout. A Kentish farmer's son who became a successful artist in comics and the film world. ISBN 525. £2.95.

OLD MAIDSTONE Vol.1 by Irene Hales. Now reprinted. ISBN 096. £2.50.

OLD MAIDSTONE Vol.2 by Irene Hales. 146 old photographs. ISBN 38X. £2.50.

OLD TONBRIDGE by Don Skinner. 146 old photographs. ISBN 398. £2.50.

OLD DEAL AND WALMER by Gregory Holyoake. 146 old photographs. ISBN 401. £2.50.

KENTISH RURAL CRAFTS & INDUSTRIES by Richard Filmer. 129 photographs showing a wide variety of rural craftsmen. ISBN 428. £2.50.

KENT TRANSPORT IN OLD POSTCARDS by Eric Baldock. 146 old photographs showing the development of all forms of transport in Kent. ISBN 320. £2.50.

VILLAGES AROUND OLD MAIDSTONE by Irene Hales. 146 old postcards. ISBN 231. £2.50.

THE CANTERBURY AND WHITSTABLE RAILWAY 1830-1980: A PICTORIAL SURVEY. (Published with the Locomotive Club of G.B.) 30 pictures and maps. ISBN 118. 75p.

MEDWAY MEMORIES by Norman Clout. A personal memory of the towns. ISBN 142. £1.50.

ROCHESTER'S HERITAGE TRAIL. (Published for The City of Rochester Society.) A useful guide for the visitor to most places of interest in Rochester. ISBN 169. £1.25.

GEORGE BARGEBRICK Esq. by Richard-Hugh Perks. The story of Smeed Dean Ltd in Sittingbourne and its colourful founder, George Smeed. 80 illustrations. ISBN 479. £2.95.

Other titles are in preparation. Details will be announced in 'Bygone Kent'.